NEGRO MEDAL OF HONOR MEN

NEGRO
MEDAL OF HONOR
MEN

☆

by Irvin H. Lee

Illustrated with photographs

DODD, MEAD & COMPANY

NEW YORK

Library of Congress Catalog Card Number: 67-11729
Printed in the United States of America
by The Cornwall Press, Inc., Cornwall, N. Y.

Portions of Chapter III appeared in *Negro Digest*
magazine in February, 1966, under the title "Negro
Heroes of the Civil War."

To
Jackie, Johnny, Pat, and Sheila

Acknowledgments

This book would not have been possible without the assistance of many fine people and the excellent resources of governmental and private agencies. Foremost, I must mention those researchers, librarians, and assistants of the Library of Congress, the New York City Public Library, the Office of Military History, the National Archives and Records Service, the Howard University Library and the Association for the Study of Negro Life and History.

My thanks also to the unheralded patriots of the U. S. Soldiers Home who related many of their combat experiences and to my Uncle Jerome Owings, who was a doughboy with the Ninety-second Division in France during World War I.

Special thanks go to Mrs. Sara D. Jackson of the Na-

Acknowledgments

tional Archives for her patience in searching for much of the material herein; to Mr. John E. Taylor and Mr. Lee Saegessers, also of the archives; to Colonel Carroll V. Glines, Captain Stewart R. Kirkpatrick, Lieutenant Colonel Richard E. Schmelz, Master Sergeant James A. George, Mr. John H. Sullivan and Mrs. Helen Burnard, for their encouragement; to Mr. James C. Evans, Counselor to the Assistant Secretary of Defense for Manpower, for his advice and assistance; to the Army, Navy, and Air Force Awards and Decorations Branches; to Senior Master Sergeant Robert C. Bueker, Headquarters, Air Training Command, for his contributions; and to Mrs. Mary Lee Stubbs, Office of Military History, who possesses a wealth of knowledge about the history of the Ninth and Tenth Cavalries.

I.H.L.

Preface

Few words in this book are devoted to the notable episodes of the American white man's fight for liberty and his maintenance of freedom at home and abroad. Volumes on this subject have been written by historians and studied by students of history over the years. In the thick of nearly every war (there are no records to show that Negroes fought in the Mexican War) in which this nation has been engaged, the Negro was there—fighting and dying just as his white comrades.

From the time colored men were integrated into the Continental Army in 1775 to the conflict in Vietnam, the Negro combatant has fought proudly. He has faced the fire of his country's foes burdened by unjustified racial prejudices. His monetary rewards were often inequitable; he frequently suffered brutality and humiliation.

In spite of these biases, the Negro, both freedmen and slaves, remained loyal to their country. Most concerned themselves with the opportunity to fight as Americans and prove their courage. These goals took precedence over being treated as "different."

The first man to give his life for American freedom was Crispus Attucks, not a soldier but a runaway Negro slave from Framingham, Massachusetts. The occasion was the historic Boston Massacre on March 5, 1770. The people had abused the king's military men beyond endurance, and the soldiers fired on a crowd. Attucks was killed by the first shot fired by the redcoats. Today on Boston Common there stands a monument erected in 1888 honoring Attucks and four other men who gave their lives for freedom that day.

During the Revolutionary War the British used charm and persuasion to induce many of the one thousand Negro enlisted troops to desert and become loyal to the crown. Instead, they maintained their devotion and supported the rebellious colonies.

After the battle of New Orleans in the War of 1812, General Andrew Jackson told Louisiana's black soldiers: "You surpassed my hopes. The nation shall applaud your valor." The praises and handclapping were neither loud nor unanimous, but the colored men were satisfied that they had served their country with honor.

Negroes served side by side with whites in integrated army and navy units from the Revolutionary struggle to the War of 1812. But from the beginning of the Civil

Preface

War to the start of the Korean conflict, Negroes fought under a "separate but equal" policy.

During these periods colored soldiers and sailors served their country faithfully, gallantly and heroically. In the face of obstacles that would have tried the courage of even the most dedicated patriot, they earned the heartfelt praise of commanders and observers.

Near the end of the War between the States, Colonel Thomas Wentworth Higginson, heroic commander of the Thirty-third Regiment, said:

"No officer in the regiment now doubts that the key to the successful prosecution of this war lies in the unlimited employment of black troops ... It would have been madness to attempt with the bravest white troops what I have successfully accomplished with the black ones."

Negroes were in the pitch of battle during the white man's engagements with the Indians. For twenty years colored cavalrymen and infantry troops fought fierce encounters with the Apaches and Sioux. They defeated Chief Victorio and captured Geronimo, paving the way for settlement of the Southwest.

From Arizona and New Mexico colored troops went to Cuba. It was there that they fought with Teddy Roosevelt's Rough Riders on San Juan Hill. "No troops could behave better than the colored soldiers," said a grateful Roosevelt after the bitter engagement.

Preface

In World Wars I and II, and later in Korea, the Negro continued to fight gallantly, with few headlines, but earning many of the nation's highest decorations for heroism. Forty-four of these black patriots earned the country's highest military award for bravery—the Medal of Honor. This book is about the valor of these men, and their comrades.

In these pages I refrain, where possible, from using "winners" in referring to award recipients. Decorations for bravery or heroism are "earned." When a man sacrifices his life for a cause all references to that effort should be elevated. The men depicted in this book, beyond a doubt, earned their awards.

I am presenting these humanitarian accounts to point out that the Negro also has the strength and foresight that a personal purpose gives. These black Americans fought, and sometimes died in battle, with no particular virtues to be glorified. The color of their skin was secondary to defending the cause they revered. But their heroism, hitherto virtually unknown, is here revealed to fill an obvious omission in U. S. military history.

The point of this book is not that colored men are different (as many of their commanders implied) from their white comrades when it comes to individual bravery. Both have courage and devotion.

I.H.L.

Contents

	Preface	*ix*
I.	The Medal of Honor	1
II.	Negroes on Korean Battlefields	9
III.	"To Save the Country . . ."	19
IV.	Negroes at Sea	35
V.	The Indian Fighters	57
VI.	Salvation at Santiago	84
VII.	Equality Achieved	99
	Appendix: *List of Negro Medal of Honor Men*	127
	Bibliography	131
	Index	133

Illustrations

Following page 78

Present Army Medal of Honor
Air Force Medal of Honor
Navy and Marine Corps Medal of Honor
Lieutenant General Benjamin O. Davis, Jr.
U. S. Colored Troops at Fort Lincoln
Colored Musicians of the Civil War
U. S. Colored Troops at Petersburg
Negro Missile Launchers
Private First Class Milton L. Olive III

NEGRO MEDAL OF HONOR MEN

Negro Medal of Honor Men

The Medal of Honor is awarded to its recipients

★

CHAPTER I

★

The Medal of Honor

THE MEDAL OF HONOR was earned only one way during World Wars I and II and the Korean conflict. This was by a deed of personal bravery or self-sacrifice, above and beyond the call of duty, performed by a member of the American Armed Forces. It was earned in actual combat with an enemy of the nation.

Apart from the great honor that it conveys, there are certain small privileges that accompany the Medal of Honor. Its recipients can, under certain conditions, obtain free military transportation. Their retirement pay, if they are enlisted men, is increased by 10 per cent. A veteran who has been awarded the medal for combat in any war is eligible, on application while on active duty, for additional pay of one hundred dollars per month. In addition, the sons of Medal of Honor men are eligible to enter U. S. military academies on a non-quota basis.

The Medal of Honor is presented to its recipients by a high official "in the name of the Congress of the United States." For this reason it is sometimes called the Congressional Medal of Honor.

On rare occasions, the Congress of the United States has awarded special Medals of Honor for individual exploits taking place in peacetime. Such medals were awarded to Captain (later Brigadier General) Charles A. Lindbergh, Major General William C. Mitchell, Commander Richard E. Byrd Jr., and others.

In the winter of 1861–62, following the beginning of hostilities in the Civil War, there was much thought in Washington about honoring the deeds of American servicemen who were distinguishing themselves in the fighting.

Congress seemed unaware that a medal had already been established to honor all brave soldiers, sailors and marines. This was the Purple Heart. George Washington created it at Newburgh, New York, on August 7, 1782, as a decoration for "singular meritorious action." Records show that only three men were awarded the Purple Heart before the 1800's.

Later, in 1847, there was a "Certificate of Merit" authorized for soldiers. The award did not provide for a medal, but only for a certificate—a document. Congress

The Medal of Honor

provided that holders of the certificate who were still in the service should have extra pay of two dollars a month; but money alone could not honor the serviceman for his deed.

And there had also been a method of honoring soldiers by means of the "brevet" system of promotions. Under this system a serviceman mentioned for gallantry in dispatches could be granted a "brevet rank" higher than that he held and be entitled to wear the insignia that went with the brevet. But this system had fallen victim to a series of political abuses, and by 1861 much of its honor had grown meaningless. It was then that Senator James W. Grimes of Iowa, as chairman of the Senate Naval Committee, took the lead in properly recognizing the nation's heroes. He introduced a bill to create a Navy Medal. It was passed by both houses of Congress and approved by President Abraham Lincoln on December 21, 1861. The law established a Medal of Honor for enlisted men of the Navy and Marine Corps.

Action on the Army Medal was started two months later, when in February, 1862, Senator Henry Wilson of Massachusetts introduced a Senate resolution. It provided for presentation of "Medals of Honor" to enlisted men of the Army and Volunteer Forces who "shall most distinguish themselves by their gallantry in action, and other soldier-like qualities."

President Lincoln's approval made the resolution law

on July 12, 1862. It was amended by an act approved on March 3, 1863, which extended its provision to include officers as well as enlisted men and made the provisions retroactive to the beginning of the Civil War.

The six survivors, none of whom were Negroes, of Major General Ormsby M. Mitchell's raid through Georgia in April, 1862, were awarded the first Army Medals of Honor on March 25, 1863, by Secretary of War Stanton. After the presentation of the medals in his office the secretary took the six to the White House for a visit with President Lincoln. A few days later, on April 3, 1863, the first Navy Medals of Honor were awarded to a number of sailors taking part in the attacks on Forts Jackson, Fisher and St. Philip on April 24, 1862.

By now the Medal of Honor had become a reality occupying the attention of many Americans. But not all the extraordinary examples of courage or service were of the type that would deserve the Medal of Honor. Yet all of them earned recognition of some sort. The problem was to determine what degree of valor or service merited the award of the Medal of Honor.

After the Civil War the number of applications for the medal for ex-soldiers increased. Many of the alleged actions had been performed long before the awards were applied for, and most lacked sound documentation. This situation led to the creation of boards of

The Medal of Honor

review, not only of individual acts, but of the whole policy involved in the award of the Medal of Honor.

One such board was later established in 1916. Between October 16, 1916, and January 17, 1917, all of the 2,625 Medals of Honor that had been awarded up to that time were reconsidered. By February 15, 1917, 911 names were stricken from the list.

Of these, 864 names were involved in one group—a case in which the medal had been given by order of Abraham Lincoln to members of a single regiment for re-enlisting. Among the remaining forty-seven who lost their medal were William F. Cody, better known as Buffalo Bill, and Mary Walker, a Civil War surgeon and the only woman ever to receive the honor. In their cases the board felt that the medal had not been properly awarded for distinguished services.

Congress on January 11, 1905, authorized a medal to be worn by all holders of the Certificate of Merit. It was given to any private soldier or noncommissioned officer "who shall distinguish himself by merit and courage" and whom the President deemed worthy of the award. The Certificate of Merit Medal was discontinued by a special Act of Congress on July 9, 1918. It was replaced by a new medal—the Distinguished Service Cross.

This decoration was brought into existence so that the status of the Medal of Honor might be more protected. The Committee on Military Affairs, which had prepared the authorization, stated that, "It is believed that if a secondary medal . . . had been authorized in the past the award of the . . . Medal of Honor would have been much more jealously guarded than it was for many years. . . ."

In addition, in 1918, Congress authorized the Navy Cross, the Distinguished Service Medals, and the Silver Star. The Purple Heart, originated by George Washington, had been revived in 1932.

The Army established two formats of the Medal of Honor before 1904. Because the originals had been copied by certain veterans' organizations, the decoration was redesigned by Major General George L. Gillespie, and the patent on the design was transferred to the Secretary of War, so that further imitations of the award could be prohibited by law.

Presently, the medal is a gold-finished star, its five points tipped by trefoils, superimposed on a laurel wreath of green enamel. In each point of the star is a green enamel oak leaf. The medallion in the center bears the head of the goddess Minerva, emblem of righteous war and wisdom, encircled by the words *United States of America*. On the reverse, above the space for the recipient's name, is the inscription *The Congress to*.

The medal is suspended from a horizontal bar bear-

The Medal of Honor

ing the word *Valor;* above it is an American eagle, wings spread, grasping laurel leaves in one claw and arrows in the other. The eagle is fastened by a hook to a ribbon or pad of light blue, studded with thirteen white stars. Since 1944 it has been given with a neck cravat of light blue, which has a star-studded light blue pad, from which the medal is extended, of octagonal shape in the center.

An Act of Congress of August 7, 1942, abolished a previous version of the Navy Medal of Honor and re-established the medal originally designed by Christian Schussel and authorized in 1862. The five-pointed bronze star, its obverse showing Minerva repulsing the figure of Discord, is identical with the original Army Medal of Honor. The reverse of the Navy Medal is blank except for the words *Personal Valor,* below which are engraved the recipient's name, rank and ship or organization and the date of the action being honored.

The medal is suspended from the flukes of an anchor, fouled by a cable; the anchor is attached by a ring at the top to an open clasp of fasces, with a five-pointed star at the center. In 1942 a ribbon suspension similar to the Army's was adopted, with a short piece of light blue ribbon folded into a square or rectangle, the traditional thirteen white stars displayed in its center, this in turn attached to a light blue neck ribbon.

Negro Medal of Honor Men

Our "Pyramid of Honor," the system of individual decorations in order of precedence, is as follows: Medal of Honor; Army Distinguished Service Cross, Navy Cross, Air Force Cross (these three equal in value); Distinguished Service Medals, Silver Star Medal, Legion of Merit, Distinguished Flying Cross; Soldier's Medal, Navy and Marine Corps Medal, Coast Guard Medal, Airman's Medal (equal in value); Bronze Star Medal, Air Medal, Air Force Combat Readiness Medal, Joint Service Commendation Medal, individual service Commendation Medals, and Purple Heart.

These decorations are followed by United States Unit Citations, U. S. Service Awards, Foreign Decorations, Foreign Unit Citations and Non-United States or Service Awards of Foreign Countries, in that order of precedence.

CHAPTER II

★

Negroes on Korean Battlefields

I<small>T</small> WAS a partly cloudy day in Washington, D.C., on June 21, 1951. The temperature outside was eighty-eight degrees. At the Pentagon, in the office of General of the Army Omar N. Bradley, Chairman of the Joint Chiefs of Staff, an aide read a citation:

"Private First Class William Thompson, 42 259 324, Company M, Twenty-fourth Infantry Regiment, distinguished himself by conspicuous gallantry and intrepidity above and beyond the call of duty in action against the enemy near Haman, Korea, on 6 August 1950. . . ."

Present at the simple, moving ceremony were General Bradley, other military men and Mrs. Mary Henderson, Private Thompson's mother. Mrs. Henderson, trying desperately not to show too much emotion, stood proud and erect as the aide neared the end of the citation:

"Private Thompson's dauntless courage and self-sacrifice reflect the highest credit on himself and uphold the esteemed traditions of the military service."

When the citation had been read, General Bradley turned slightly and presented a posthumous award of the Medal of Honor to Mrs. Henderson. In presenting the medal the general expressed the nation's pride in her son's heroism. The award had been earned by her twenty-two-year-old son, who had died a hero on August 6, 1950, while defending an outpost near Haman, Korea.

Private Thompson was a Negro and the first of his race since 1898 to earn the Medal of Honor for martyrdom above and beyond the call of duty. He and, later, Sergeant Cornelius H. Charlton were the only Negroes to be so honored for heroism during the Korean conflict.

Thompson was a Brooklyn boy, who experienced hardship early in life. Before entering the Army in 1945, the youngster was a waif at the New York Home for Homeless Boys. He had been taken there by a solicitous minister, who reportedly found him sleeping in a park.

Thompson was drafted two months after his eighteenth birthday. On February 25, 1947, after almost a year and a half of army duty, he was honorably discharged and went back to New York. Those who knew him said he found it difficult to adjust to civilian life, so he reenlisted in the Regular Army on June 14, 1948. Sixteen days later he arrived at Inchon, Korea, with Company M of the Twenty-fourth Infantry Regiment, Twenty-fifth Infantry Division.

Thompson was with M Company's First Platoon. The unit was a part of a task force rushed to Korea to divert North Korean attacks aimed at Taegu along the Taejon-Taegu Road.

On August 6, 1948, just ten days from his twenty-third birthday, Thompson's platoon was reorganizing under cover of darkness near Haman. Suddenly, fanatical enemy forces in overwhelming strength launched a surprise attack on the platoon. Thompson, who had been awarded the Army's coveted Combat Infantryman Badge, set up his machine gun in the path of the attackers. Immediately he swept the enemy with withering gunfire that momentarily halted the advance. His action slowed the charge long enough to permit a portion of the platoon to take defensive positions in the midst of exploding grenades and a devastating hail of enemy gunfire.

Thompson was hit by grenade fragments and small arms fire during the attack, but that didn't seem to

11

matter to him. Though badly wounded he remained at his post, spraying enemy positions with machine-gun fire. At one point he refused orders to withdraw and resisted efforts of comrades to remove him by physical force.

"Maybe I won't get out," he reportedly yelled to one noncommissioned officer, "but I'm gonna take a lot of 'em with me." With that he released another burst from his machine gun and continued to fire, until he was mortally wounded by an exploding enemy grenade.

Private Thompson was not the first Negro of the Twenty-fourth Infantry to receive the Medal of Honor. In 1890, sixty-one years before, Sergeant Benjamin Brown and Corporal Isaiah Mays earned the medal during a fight with robbers in Arizona. At that time the Twenty-fourth was, except for its commanding officers, an all-Negro unit.

In 1948, President Harry S. Truman, as Commander-in-Chief of the Armed Forces, issued an executive order to promote "the highest standards of democracy" among our fighting men. The legal effect of this was to nullify "separate but equal" recruitment, training and service.

Integration was slow, but in the early 1950's it became a practical necessity. The Korean crisis brought an immediate swelling of the armed forces. This, plus the policy of replacing individual troops in Korea by regular rotation, gradually eliminated segregation. For

Negroes on Korean Battlefields

the first time, the Negro was permitted to fight as an integrated member of a combat unit.

In July, 1950, a month before Private Thompson's heroism near Haman, two Negroes had already earned the nation's second highest award for valor—the Distinguished Service Cross. They were Second Lieutenants William H. Benefield, Jr. and William D. Ware.

Benefield was from Kansas City, Missouri, and went to Korea as a member of the Seventy-seventh Combat Engineer Company. Less than two weeks after his arrival he was killed by enemy fire while attempting to clear a minefield near Sanju. On the same day Lieutenant Ware, a Texan, earned the Distinguished Service Cross for gallantry near Sangju. He was a member of the historic Twenty-fourth Infantry. His citation reads in part:

"The position was attacked from three sides by numerically superior enemy forces armed with automatic weapons and supported by mortar fire. . . . Lieutenant Ware, arming himself with a rifle, ordered his men to withdraw. He was last seen firing . . . on the advancing enemy until his position was overrun."

In August, 1950, another Texan, Master Sergeant Levy V. Hollis, won the Distinguished Service Cross near Haman. Three months later a North Carolinian, First Lieutenant Ellison C. Wynn, also earned the nation's second highest award for valor. As Commander of

Negro Medal of Honor Men

B Company, Ninth Infantry Regiment, he led his troops in an assault on an enemy position near Kuni-ri.

During a counterattack, the officer's machine gunners were killed, but he remained at his post throwing grenades until his men could rejoin him in defending the position. Although bleeding from wounds, Wynn staunchly directed a withdrawal.

Later, on December 4 of the same year, a white officer earned the Medal of Honor for risking his life to save a Negro. Lieutenant Thomas J. Hudner, Jr. of Massachusetts attempted to rescue Ensign Jesse L. Brown after his plane was shot down over North Korea. Brown, a native of Mississippi, was the first Negro to earn his wings as a naval aviator. He was assigned to the U.S.S. *Leyte.*

Brown crashed near the Chosin Reservoir and was trapped alive in the burning wreckage. Hudner landed wheels-up on the rough mountainous terrain, though enemy troops were in the area. It was subzero weather. In spite of the hazards, the white officer, with his bare hands, packed the fuesalge with snow to keep the flames away from the trapped pilot and struggled to pull him free. Unsuccessful in this, he returned to his crashed aircraft and radioed other planes, requesting a helicopter be dispatched with an ax and fire extinguisher. In the meantime, he remained near Brown's plane despite an approaching enemy force. Hudner and a rescue pilot

Negroes on Korean Battlefields

later renewed a desperate but unavailing battle against time, cold and flames.

Six months later, on June 2, 1951, Sergeant Cornelius H. Charlton earned the Medal of Honor for "conspicuous gallantry and intrepidity above and beyond the call of duty in action against the enemy near Chipo-ri, Korea."

Sergeant Charlton was one of seventeen children born to the Van Charltons at East Gulf, West Virginia. "Connie," as he was known by friends, was a quiet and gentle young man. His six-foot, two-hundred-pound frame might have been an asset to any collegiate football team.

He enlisted in the Regular Army on November 2, 1946, after the family moved to the Bronx, New York. On March 8, 1950, Charlton left the United States for service with the Far East Command, which was headquartered in Tokyo, Japan. Seven months later he was sent to Korea with Company C, Twenty-fourth Infantry Regiment, Twenty-fifth Infantry Division. He was a replacement and in the eight months of combat there had advanced to the rank of sergeant, earning several campaign medals, including the Korean Service Medal with four Bronze Service Stars.

The Twenty-fourth was a seasoned combat unit. It had won impressive battles in Korea. After the regiment's victory at Battle Mountain, Sergeant Charlton was made a platoon leader with an element of C Com-

15

pany, First Battalion. On June 2, 1951, Charlton's unit was in the fourth day of an assault against heavily fortified Hill 542 near Chipo-ri.

His platoon was attacking a reinforced Chinese Communist position when the enemy opened fire on his men with automatic weapons. Several soldiers and the white officer in command of the integrated unit fell wounded. They were later evacuated. Charlton, just twenty-one years old, assumed command and led a handful of troops up a steep hill to wipe out the enemy stronghold. In the initial advance he personally destroyed two positions with grenades and rifle fire, killing six Chinese soldiers.

When most of the Communist strongholds were reduced, the courageous Negro regrouped his men and led them with all deliberate speed in another assault to the top of the enemy-held hill. A rain of enemy grenades exploded about them, staggering the advance and wounding many men. Once more he regrouped the soldiers and led them forward only to be again hurled back by a shower of grenades. One of the bursts struck Sergeant Charlton severely in the chest. Yet he saw to it that the wounded were removed, then gathered his troops for another assault.

His comrades pleaded with him to have his wound treated, but he refused and continued the advance. The assault ended successfully near the crest of the ridge, but a remaining enemy group prevented them from going further.

Charlton, his chest bleeding heavily now, charged the position in a one-man assault. As he approached the stronghold, grenades exploded about him. One went off at his feet, but with his last strength he fired a burst from his weapon, killing and routing the defenders before he died. The sergeant had eliminated the obstacle, and his troops finally took Hill 542.

Van and Clara Charlton, the sergeant's parents, received the posthumously awarded Medal of Honor for Charlton's heroism during that June 2 victory. Secretary of the Army Frank Pace, Jr. made the presentation at the Pentagon on March 12, 1952. Looking on during the ceremony were three of Sergeant Charlton's brothers, Thomas, Chester and Macio, and a sister, Dephnia.

For "his indomitable courage, superb leadership, and gallant self-sacrifice" Sergeant Cornelius H. Charlton became the forty-third Negro to win the highest military award for bravery given to any individual by the United States.

Lieutenant Luther M. McManus was one of the last Negroes to earn the Distinguished Service Cross during the Korean conflict. The Washington, D.C. native was cited for gallantry near Wolbong-ni on October 18, 1951. McManus fearlessly led a platoon of the Twenty-

Negro Medal of Honor Men

first Infantry in a determined charge against a hostile
position.

The Negro, living and fighting for the first time with
white combatants during the Korean conflict, proved he
had the resolution and sagacity displayed by his fore-
fathers.

★

CHAPTER III

★

"To Save the Country..."

SEGREGATION IN THE MILITARY made its debut during the Civil War. Yet there were 209,511 colored soldiers and seamen, freedmen and slaves, fighting on the Union side during the War between the States. Sixteen of them earned the Medal of Honor for their valor.

General Nathaniel P. Banks, Commander, Department of the Gulf, said in referring to the Negroes' combat behavior: "It gives me great pleasure to report that they answered every expectation. Their conduct was heroic; no troops could be more determined or more daring."

Banks, a Union officer who led his forces victoriously at Shenandoah Valley, Virginia; New Orleans, Louisiana; and Mobile Bay, Alabama; was referring to the gallantry and martyrdom of his Negro troops.

19

Negro Medal of Honor Men

This was but one of the many praises bestowed on Negro infantrymen who fought in the Civil War. And they not only fought. They fought gallantly, sometimes displaying a sheer heroism that naturally caused the nation to seek an unprecedented means of rewarding them.

Most of the Civil War's colored combatants were contraband—slaves who escaped from their masters to the Union lines. Others were freedmen, those who had been released from slavery. General Benjamin F. Butler, the first to call escaped slaves "contraband of war," made the initial effort to deal with them at Fort Monroe in 1861. At the time there were no provisions for their use as combat troops. So he, and later General Ulysses S. Grant, used them to build roads and fortifications. This discriminate use of valuable manpower caused considerable controversy in the North. Most citizens believed that all available men should be used directly in the war effort.

In July, 1862, Congress, in eliminating racial restrictions, said simply that the enrollment of militia should include all able-bodied male citizens between the ages of eighteen and forty-five. The Emancipation Proclamation, issued on September 22, 1862, favored arming freed slaves. Less than four weeks after it was issued, Secretary of War Stanton authorized the governor of Massachusetts to enlist Negro volunteers. Governor John Andrews spearheaded the movement to raise the

"To Save the Country . . ."

Massachusetts Fifty-fourth U. S. Colored Infantry, the first Negro regiment recruited in the North. One member of the Fifty-fourth, Sergeant William H. Carney, later became the first of his race to earn the Medal of Honor.

Rhode Island had the distinction of organizing the first colored artillery regiment in the North. As early as August 4, 1862, the governor of the state had issued the call for a regiment to consist "entirely of colored citizens."

Almost two months later, on October 28, 1862, the Seventy-ninth Colored Infantry (First Kansas) became the first Negro regiment to be engaged in combat. The action took place at Island Mounds, Missouri.

On February 6, 1863, Frederick Douglass, an escaped slave and Negro abolitionist, asked Governor Andrew Curtin of Pennsylvania if he would accept colored troops. The governor's answer was no. But General Robert E. Lee's invasion of southeastern Pennsylvania in the early summer of 1863 had alarmed the state and made many of its citizens less hostile to the idea of blacks in blue. Weeks later a committee of prominent civic leaders in Philadelphia secured authorization to recruit Negro soldiers. On June 23, 1863, Camp William Penn, near Philadelphia, received its first eighty Negro recruits.

Other commonwealths in the North—Connecticut,

Michigan, Ilinois, Indiana, Iowa and Kansas—raised one or more regiments of colored troops, but state efforts were soon slowed by sheer lack of numbers. There were simply not enough Negroes above the Mason-Dixon line.

To relieve the problem, on March 25, 1863, Adjutant General Lorenzo Thomas was dispatched from Washington to the Mississippi Valley with orders to recruit as many Negroes for combat as possible. He visited centers where Negroes were congregated, addressing them and urging them to rally to the flag. "They eagerly seek to enter military organization," he wrote from Milliken's Bend, Louisiana.

In a matter of months so many Negro troops had been recruited that on May 22, 1863, a Bureau of Colored Troops was necessary. Headed by Thomas, it was established in Washington to handle all matters pertaining to the recruitment, organization and service of Negro regiments.

Two months later Congress took action to broaden recruitment. It passed a conscription act that authorized northern governors to send agents into the Confederate states to recruit Negroes.

By the end of the year, a total of 20,790 Negro volunteers had been recruited in the valley of the Mississippi —825 in the cavalry, 4,517 in the artillery and 15,448 in the infantry. By fall an additional ten thousand were trained and ready for the smoke and din of skirmish.

"To Save the Country . . ."

Negroes trained and fought on a segregated basis and were not treated as equal with whites. For example, the Negro soldier received seven dollars' pay a month, but whites received thirteen. Because of this unequal treatment many of the colored soldiers became restive, sullen and even insubordinate. But the majority were less interested in being treated differently than in having the opportunity to fight and prove their courage and devotion.

Sergeant Major Christian A. Fleetwood, a handsome, one-hundred-twenty-five-pound Baltimore free Negro, perhaps best exemplified the Negroes' motivation when he said he had enlisted "to save the country from ruin."

After serving with Union forces at Yorktown, Pennsylvania, and Fort Fisher, North Carolina, Fleetwood expressed the feelings of most colored men as he wrote in his diary: "This year has brought about many changes that at the beginning were or would have been thought impossible. The close of the year finds me a soldier for the cause of my race. May God bless the cause, and enable me in the coming year to forward it on." He did, for nine months later his courage earned him a Medal of Honor.

The flag—Confederate and Union—served as a rallying point for both sides during the Civil War. In the North, John Adams Dix, just after taking office as Secretary of the Treasury, issued his famous "American Flag

Dispatch." He said: "If any man attempts to haul down the American flag, shoot him on the spot."

Dix's message typifies the spirit of Negro color-bearers who sacrificed their lives protecting the Stars and Stripes during the War of the Rebellion.

Sergeant William H. Carney, Company C, Fifty-fourth Massachusetts Colored Infantry, was one of those who faced death on the battlefield for the sake of the flag. He was the first Negro in the Civil War to earn the Medal of Honor.

Born in Norfolk, Virginia, in 1840, at fourteen he had attended a private and secret school supervised by a minister. "In my fifteenth year," he wrote, "I embraced the gospel." Later he ran away from his master's farm to become a seaman. He finally settled in New Bedford, Massachusetts. There young Carney did odd jobs for a living while still retaining his preference for the Christian ministry. When the call went out for Negro infantrymen "to save the Union," Carney, twenty-three years old, enlisted on February 17, 1863.

The sergeant earned his medal five months later at Fort Wagner, South Carolina, a point vital to the capture of Charleston. Here he and his fellow patriots bore one of their severest tests of valor.

The weather was perfect. It was about noon on July 18, 1863. Union land batteries opened cannon fire from the south and were joined simultaneously by six ironclads. Within about a thousand yards of the fort the Negroes stopped their advance and lay flat on the ground waiting for the order to charge.

The signal was given. At the command "Attention" the men stood up, and the metallic tones of the bugle sounded the advance. Into the storm of fire the Fifty-fourth moved, in double-time, past the southeastern defenses of the fort, into the deep ditch before it, up and over the bulwark, into Wagner itself.

Carney had advanced but a short distance when musketry fire and shells exploded about him, wounding or killing about a dozen men on his right and left. One of those wounded was Sergeant John Wall, the color-bearer. Before the flag slipped from Wall's relaxing fingers, Sergeant Carney sprang forward and seized it. He then made his way to the head of the column.

His advance was slowed by the enemy's fire. In less than twenty minutes Carney found himself alone at the fort's entrance. Around him lay the dead and wounded as they had fallen one on another. He dared not enter the fort alone, so still holding the flag, he hid at its outer slope. Sand flew in his face as musket shells and grenades hit the ground around him.

After half an hour the Union forces renewed their attack to the right, and the enemy's attention was drawn from him. As he started to run through the smoke a group of soldiers came advancing toward him. As they approached, Carney raised his flag and was about to join them when he suddenly realized that they were rebels. Hurriedly winding the colors around the staff, he turned down an embankment into a ditch with water that came to his waist. Carney was alone again.

Carney continued his flight to the rear and was shot twice. This did not deter him. He struggled on, clutching the flag as he stumbled. On the way, he met a member of the One-hundredth New York. The New Yorker treated the sergeant's wounds, and they retreated to the rear. As the two dodged enemy fire, Carney was wounded by a shot that grazed his head. He stumbled from the hit, and the rescuer offered to carry the flag. Carney refused, saying: "No one but a member of the Fifty-fourth should carry the colors."

When the two reached Union lines, Sergeant Carney was treated by medical corpsmen, then went to his regimental encampment. When his comrades saw him carrying the flag, they cheered, and he said: "The flag never touched the ground, boys." Carney was discharged from the infantry at Black Island, South Carolina, on June 30, 1864, with disability caused by the wounds he had received.

Meanwhile, when General Grant left the West to take command of the Union army and direct the fighting on the crucial Virginia front, he insisted on bringing twenty thousand Negro infantrymen.

"To Save the Country . . ."

"The Negro," said Sergeant Major Fleetwood of the Virginia campaigns, "stood in the full glare of the greatest searchlight, part and parcel of the grandest armies ever mustered upon this continent, competing side by side with the bravest and best of Lee's army, and losing nothing by comparison."

At Deep Bottom, Virginia, on July 21, 1864, four black regiments, Pennsylvania's Sixth U. S. Colored Troops among them, fought with intrepidity in one of the fiercest campaigns of the battle for Virginia. The Negro volunteers defiantly withstood the enemy assault; outstanding among them was Sergeant Major Thomas Hawkins.

Hawkins, though born in Cincinnati, enlisted in the Union Army on August 4, 1863 at Philadelphia. He was awarded the Medal of Honor for gallantry in rescuing the regimental flag during the Deep Bottom engagement. Of the action, in which about three hundred Negroes died, Major General D. B. Birney, Tenth Corps Commander, said: "It was one of the most stirring and gallant affairs I have ever known."

Sergeant Decatur Dorsey also earned his Medal of Honor for saving the colors. At Petersburg, about seven-thirty on the morning of July 30, 1864, the reserve brigades of Negro troops were sent into battle after an assault by whites had failed. Faced by musketry fire in front, a cross fire of shells from the flanks and white troops retreating in their direction, the Negroes began the charge.

Dorsey, a member of Maryland's Thirty-ninth U. S. Colored Troops, moved forward and mounted his flag on Confederate soil in advance of his regiment. Seeing their flag ahead, the Union forces advanced daringly in spite of heavy casualties. Their effort was in vain. The Confederate defenders stubbornly held their positions and drove the Union troops back to their lines.

Dorsey carried the flag in the retreat, then rallied the men in a new assault. Later, the Negroes moved over the rebel defenses and engaged the enemy in close combat, taking two stands of colors and two hundred prisoners for the only (but temporary) success of the day. After a second assault Major General Ambrose Burnside, corps commander, ordered a retreat because "the men were largely without leaders" and had become disorganized. The Negro brigade's casualty list of 1,324 was greater than that of any other of the three attacking divisions.

The number of colored troops engaged in Virginia in the last twelve months of the war was impressive. Thirteen Negro regiments fought at Chaffin's Farm, New Market Heights and Fort Harrison at the end of September. A total of thirty-seven Medals of Honor were awarded to participants in that two-day struggle, thirteen of which went to members of colored organizations.

"To Save the Country . . ."

On September 29 and 30, 1864, the Negroes confirmed their well-earned reputation for gallantry. At the gray of dawn on the twenty-ninth they moved steadily but slowly up to surrounding fortifications at New Market Heights. As the nine infantry regiments advanced, the assault columns were repeatedly struck with shell and grenades. But they pressed on. The rebels began to retreat as the overwhelming Union forces moved in. General Birney had ordered the Negroes to take the fort at bayonet point, but the rebels fled under heavy fire without waiting for the charge.

The Negroes swept over the main fortification and took possession. The first to enter were First Sergeant Edward Ratcliff. Sergeant James H. Harris and Private William H. Barnes, all of New Jersey's Thirty-eighth U. S. Colored Troops, and Private James Gardiner of the Thirty-sixth. All earned Medals of Honor for bravery and daring in the assault. Gardiner rushed ahead of his brigade during the attack, shot a rebel officer who was rallying his men, then ran him through with his bayonet.

Courageous men like Ratcliff, Harris, Barnes and Gardiner were responsible for the Union victory—at the cost of one thousand casualties. General Benjamin Butler, riding along the line of charge, counted 543 dead bodies in a space of three hundreds yards long and "not wider than the clerk's desk." Later he wrote, "As I rode among the victorious, jubilant colored troops at New Market Heights, I felt in my inmost heart that the

29

capacity of the Negro race for soldiers had then and there been fully settled forever."

Meanwhile, at Chaffin's Farm the men of the Fourth, Fifth, and Sixth U. S. Colored Troops were fighting what one observer called the "bloodiest battle of the War between the States." The Fourth and Sixth lost more than half their men in one encounter.

A regiment lined up for the charge with 11 officers and 350 enlisted men. Major A. S. Boernstein, the only field officer, was in command. Regimental Adjutant George Allen supervised the right and Sergeant Major Fleetwood the left. When the charge began there were twelve color-bearers. Only one of them came off the field on his feet. The others were killed or wounded.

"Early in the rush," according to Medal of Honor winner Fleetwood's account, "one of the sergeants went down, a bullet cutting his flag staff in two and passing through his body. The other sergeant, Alfred B. Hilton of Company H, Maryland's Fourth U. S. Colored Troops, a magnificent specimen of manhood, over 6 ft. tall and splendidly proportioned, caught the other flag and pressed forward with both of them."

The Confederates continued to bombard the Union forces with musketry fire and shells. Men fell "as hail-stones sweep the leaves from the trees," Fleetwood wrote in his diary. During the advance, Hilton was shot through the leg. As he fell, he held up the flags and shouted: "Boys, save the colors!" On October 21, twenty days after his daring rescue, Sergeant Hilton died of his wounds.

Before the flag could touch the ground, Private Charles Veal of D Company seized the blue flag and Fleetwood the Stars and Stripes, which had been presented to the regiment by a group of patriotic women when the Fourth U. S. Colored Troops left Baltimore in late 1863.

The rebel fortress proved to be quite a bastion for the Union forces. There were strong embankments, protected in front by two barricades of felled trees with pointed branches and a row of pointed stakes embedded in the ground. Behind these defenses waited experienced marksmen, who outnumbered the attackers. The obstacles were too strong for the Union soldiers, and those that were able fled back to their lines.

After reaching a contingent of reserves, Fleetwood saw there was no commissioned officer to lead another assault. He rallied more than thirty-five survivors around the flag in one final effort to capture the fort.

Of the engagement, Fleetwood said:

"I have never been able to understand how Veal and I lived under such a hail of bullets, unless it was because we were both such little fellows. I think I weighed then about 125 pounds and Veal about the same. We did not get a scratch. A bullet passed between my legs, cutting my boot leg trousers and even my stockings, without breaking the skin."

Sergeants Fleetwood and Hilton and Private Veal were awarded Medals of Honor for their courage and intrepidity during that battle. A member of the Sixth U. S. Colored Troops, First Sergeant Alexander Kelly of Company F, also received the medal for action during that encounter. He saved the regimental flag after the color-bearer and most of his unit had been killed or wounded.

The victories at Chaffin's Farm, costly in terms of human life, were more than just conquests. They did much to prove the courage, dedication and ability of the Negro soldier. They also proved his valor in spite of obstacles and his ability to lead.

Most of the Negro units were commanded by whites; there were only seventy-five Negro officers, including eight physicians, serving in the Civil War. There was no possibility of advancement for enlisted men into the ranks of commissioned officers. This did not mean that the colored combatants did not possess leadership qualities. They did. This also was pointed out at Chaffin's Farm on September 29, 1864.

There Negro enlisted men gallantly led their men after their commanding officers were killed or wounded. Four members of Ohio's Fifth U. S. Colored Troops won

Medals of Honor for commanding their fellow enlisted men in engagements at the farm.

Ohio was one of the states that stubbornly refused to arm Negroes. Those who volunteered for service as soldiers were restricted to building defenses around the state, particularly in Cincinnati. But when that city was threatened in September, 1862, by the invasion of Confederates in nearby Kentucky, the mayor ordered the Negroes pressed into service for combat. Thus was organized the Fifth.

Its men never expected to see action. Yet on September 29 the unit's casualty rate for that day was 236—28 killed, 185 wounded and 23 captured or missing.

Nearly all of the unit's officers were disabled that day. But four highly capable noncommissioned officers—Sergeant Major Milton M. Holland, nineteen years old; First Sergeants James H. Bronson, twenty-six; Robert Pinn, twenty-one; and Powhatan Beaty, twenty-five— were left in command of their respective companies. Each earned a Medal of Honor for gallantry and meritoriously leading his unit through the day's bloody struggles.

During the final offensive of this two-day battle at Chaffin's Farm, another Negro earned one of the last Medals of Honor awarded during the Civil War. Corporal Miles James exemplified the Negroes' courage as the troops held their ground and inflicted great punishment on the enemy. James took his position within thirty yards of rebel territory. A musket shot mutilated one of his arms, yet he loaded and fired his weapon with one hand. In spite of continuous pleas to have the shattered arm treated, he urged the men of the Thirty-sixth U. S. Colored Troops to press the assault. His stirring action rallied the troops, and the enemy was routed and beaten off with heavy losses.

General Butler was so proud of his colored troops he had two hundred medals made by Tiffany's and presented them to Negro soldiers for their performance in the storming of New Market Heights and Chaffin's Farm. The first of forty-six Butler Medals was presented in May, 1865. It is suspended by a red, white and blue ribbon. The obverse of the silver medal shows a bastion being charged by two Negro soldiers. The bottom bears the inscription "U. S. Colored Troops." The reverse has an oak wreath surrounding the inscription "Campaign Before Richmond" in four lines. The whole is encircled by the words "Distinguished for Courage" and two stars.

What happened in this two-day engagement or series of engagements at Chaffin's Farm was more than the sum of enormous Union casualties. The territory gained was held until the close of the war, and the campaign of 1864 in Virginia, opened so brilliantly and successfully by Negro troops, was closed with equal valor and prowess.

Negro Medal of Honor Men

★

CHAPTER IV

★

Negroes at Sea

I T was just after midnight on December 25, 1863. The U. S. S. Gunboat *Marblehead* was anchored in the Stone River a little above Legáreville, South Carolina. The gunboat was in the six-hundred-ton class, with a paddle wheel on each side. Mounted on the maintop, near the bow, were Parrott guns. Four twenty-inch brass Dahlgren cannon were ranged along her sides.

Around the rifles and cannon crewmen, both white and colored, were busy preparing to launch a surprise attack on rebel positions on nearby John's Island. All over the ship men were ready for the attack—in the main top, crews were checking the armament; some distance away powderboys were loading gunpowder boxes. In Lieutenant Commander Richard W. Meade, Jr.'s quarters, Robert Blake, Meade's steward, was going

about his domestic chores as the commander lay half
asleep in his berth.

At five that morning a howitzer shell fired from the
island rocked the ship. The roaring concussion sent the
crew scrambling for cover. The commander sat up,
jumped from his berth and ran, still wearing his night-
clothes, to his battle station on the quarterdeck. Behind
him came Blake, waving the commander's uniform.

"Mistah Meade, Mistah Meade," he pleaded, "Yah
clos'."

Now more shells rocked the ship. Meade mounted the
quarterdeck to take a quick look at the situation. Blast
by blast the crashing, rending howitzer shells came
closer. A near direct hit exploded not far from the starboard. Struggling to put on his uniform, Meade yelled:
"Man the guns. Commence firing."

With that the *Marblehead*'s artillery opened fire. The
battle had begun. Blake left the commander's station
and went to the gun deck. As he arrived, a shell
slammed into the hull a few feet away, hurling a powderboy through the air. Blake was knocked to the deck.
Dazed and bruised but still intact, he saw the powderboy sprawled on the deck. He was splattered with
blood. Blake checked and saw that he was dead.

In the excitement and pending danger, Blake could
have returned to the relative safety of his quarters. But
he didn't. Sacrificing his comfort and immediate self-

interest, he decided to take the dead powderboy's place. Someone had to carry the gunpowder boxes to assure equal distribution of the explosive substance to the gun crews.

Blake immediately stripped to the waist and joined the fight. He repeatedly grabbed gunpowder boxes and ran with them to the gun loaders. His activity was like that of a seasoned veteran. Little did he resemble the faithful servant whose profession was cooking, cleaning and attending the personal needs of his commander.

Shell fragments thudded against the ship's deck in a tight pattern. Some fell about six inches over his head. He crouched, maintaining his speed, fearlessly dashing to gun positions and the powder magazine. As fast as he could move, he carried the boxes with unbelievable care.

On one occasion, a shell exploded broadside not far from the powder magazine. Water spewed over the deck just as Blake arrived at the spot. Cautiously he ran over the slippery area, falling once to one knee and at the same time maintaining a firm grip on the box to avoid spilling the powder and causing a possible explosion if it was ignited.

When the gunners became tense, Blake, while standing to the rear of the guns with the box under his left arm and the cover held closed with his right, attempted to relieve the anxiety. With a broad grin on his black face, his body erect between loadings, he made humorous remarks while passing the powder with almost the same grace he used when serving Commander Meade's meals.

At one point the commander visited the gun deck to inspect the crew. On seeing Blake, he asked what he was doing. Blake's reply: "Went down to the rocks to hide my face, the rocks cried out no hiding place, so har I is, suh." With that he ran off to the powder magazine. Meade smiled, shook his head in amazement, then returned to the quarter deck.

A little after seven that Christmas evening the howitzers on John's Island had stopped firing. The rebels had been defeated. Blake, though exhausted, hurried off to Meade's quarters. In the background, almost unnoticed by the cheering gun crews, a loader remarked:

"Blackie worked with such fearlessness and good nature that we were compelled to laugh and cheer when he appeared with his boxes. He lifted our spirits."

Three days later, when the commander went ashore to plant the Union flag, Blake was given the major credit for the victory. Of his activity the commander said, "He excited my admiration by the cool and brave manner in which he served the guns."

On April 16, 1864, the courageous ex-slave was awarded the Navy Medal of Honor for "conspicuous gallantry, extraordinary heroism, and intrepidity at the risk of his own life." He became the first colored seaman in history to be so honored, though Negroes had long served as sailors.

Since early in the seventeenth century Negroes, both free and slave, had held close ties to the sea. They were widely employed as privateers (merchant seamen who raided ships during a war) and on trading and fishing ships. Colored masters or ship's captains were also well known and plentiful in coastal trade. In fact, many of the most noted Negroes of the eighteenth and nineteenth centuries earned livelihoods, at some point in their careers, at sea.

The only Negroes in the War of 1812 were freedmen from Louisiana. They played conspicuous roles in the naval engagements of that war—composing from 10 to 20 per cent of the crews. Commodore Oliver Hazard Perry, early in the encounters, called a group of replacements sent him "a motley set—blacks, soldiers, boys," but he was satisfied to get "anything in the shape of a man." At the end of the Battle of Lake Erie in 1813, his words were different. Of his numerous colored crewmen he said, "They seemed absolutely insensible to danger."

During the Civil War the Union Navy maintained its rule of nondiscrimination aboard ships. When manpower became scarce it began signing up fugitive slaves, a policy never before established.

"Fill up the crews with contraband obtained from Major General John Adams Dix," ordered Navy Secretary

Negro Medal of Honor Men

Gideon Welles. "There is not an available sailor North." Welles's order was directed to Commodore Charles Wilks, who was commander of the James River flotilla. General Dix was commander of Fort Monroe, a haven for escaped slaves.

Contrabands like Blake responded in impressive numbers to the Navy's beckoning. Even veteran Negro seamen whose terms were about to expire agreed to continue their service. Many of the new recruits signed up because of the Navy's policy of equal treatment; others because they did not want to expose themselves elsewhere to militant segregationist thinking.

During the War between the States as many as 29,000 Negroes (one-fourth of the entire naval strength) served with the Union fleet. At least forty-nine vessels had colored crewmen who were killed, captured or wounded in action. Their casualties numbered an estimated eight hundred, approximately one-quarter of the Navy total of 3,220 victims. To these statistics must be added another estimated two thousand colored seamen who died of disease.

The Navy has its roster of unsung blacks who discharged their duties courageously, but few were acclaimed national heroes. Of the 729 Navy Medals of Honor awarded since 1862, only seven went to Negro seamen. Four earned the medal during the Civil War, two for heroism in 1872 and 1898 and one during the Spanish-American War.

Negroes at Sea

The nation's highest medal for heroism at sea is designed much like the one authorized for wear by heroes of the Army. The only difference is that the Navy's medal is attached by an anchor.

Perhaps the most striking quality of these Negro Medal of Honor winners is not the color of their skin or that they risked death, but that they never lost their sense of concern and responsibility for fellow crewmen and the Union. Their backgrounds are so obscure that history and military records in most cases list only the place and date of birth. Yet, the stories of these seven men are epics of courage and gallantry.

Blake enlisted in the Federal Navy after escaping from a Virginia plantation. He was one of the first to volunteer after Secretary Welles authorized the employment of contrabands on Union vessels.

The ex-slave was a disciplined, compulsively hard worker and very dark-complexioned. The "black as night" texture of his skin earned him the nickname "Blackie." But he took the name honorably, and the crew used it with affection.

Blake had personality and poise. These characteristics stood uppermost in the minds of his fellow crewmen. Nothing seemed to bother him. No matter how demanding the assignment, he managed to proceed faithfully, energetically and with a positive disposition.

On Christmas Day, 1863, his manner and courage earned for him an accolade of a grateful nation. His courage aboard the *Marblehead* was not only deserving of the Medal of Honor, but it made a mockery of the theory that slaves were worthless except in the fields.

Almost six months and thousands of miles later another Negro added impetus to Commodore Perry's statement that the colored seaman "seemed absolutely insensible to danger."

He was Joachim Pease, a native of Long Island, New York, who had never known slavery. Pease was a veteran Navy man, having been promoted, because of his proficiency, from landsman to seaman in a relatively short period of time.

Any experienced sailor could look at Pease's muscular chest and arms and tell he was a loader of some kind. Yet the bronze complexion of his skin immediately ruled out the possibility of his being a stoker. The upper half of Pease's body was sunburned from being exposed while working on the upper deck.

Pease was a gun loader aboard the U. S. S. *Kearsarge*. The vessel, commanded by Captain John A. Wilson, was 1,031 tons and had an integrated crew of 162, and 8 guns, the first of which was loaded by Seaman Pease.

The *Kearsarge* lay off Cherbourg, France, when the famous battle between her and the rebel commerce-destroyer *Alabama* took place on June 18, 1864. The Confederate vessel was the best ship the South had. In her career she had sunk, burned or captured sixty-nine ships. Her crew was justly proud of that record, and they were confident that the *Kearsarge* would be her seventieth victim.

The Confederate victory, if there was to be one, would not come easy. The *Kearsarge's* crewmen were a determined lot, and morale aboard the ship was high. It had men like Pease, who was said to be one of the best men on the ship. Pease's gun crew included Seaman James H. Lee, a sponger from New York City, and Captain of the Top Robert Strahan, who commanded the Number One gunners.

Pease, as gun loader, held the most important position on the gun deck. Spongers, who cooled the artillery pieces after each firing, ranked second in status. Their jobs were demanding and required composure in addition to physical strength. Pease possessed these qualities.

The duel between the *Kearsarge* and the *Alabama* lasted a little longer than ninety minutes. It was bitter, and both ships took a pounding. The *Alabama's* shells were falling faster and closer. One landed within several yards of Pease, knocking three men to the deck. One man sat up looking with amazement at his bleeding hand and arm; another raised his head with blood running from his mouth and ears from the concussion, and a third lay lifeless.

To Pease, the sight of those three men was too much. He had to keep his gun going. Now he and Lee began working with unbelievable precision. As soon as the boy handed him the powder box, he put the charge in the cannon. It fired, sending deadly shells at the *Alabama*. Every four or five minutes the Number One gun unleashed devastating projectiles upon the rebel vessel. At times Lee barely had enough time to cool the cannon.

At one point, as though the rebels were determined to knock out Pease's crew, a shell landed within a few feet of his position. The explosion showered them with shrapnel. Pease and Lee were stunned but unhurt.

Jumping to his feet, Pease yelled, "Powder!" The boy arrived with his box, the Negro loaded the cannon and a retaliatory shell was hurled toward its target.

"We'll show 'em, huh Jim?" Pease said to his sponger.

"Those damn rebels," he replied. "They think . . ."

"Powder!" Pease again demanded. Again he and Lee unleashed a devastating shell.

They worked this way, yelling and firing, talking it up in a frenzied rhythm, performing in their own private hell.

Then, as quickly as it had begun, the fight was over. from the deck of the *Kearsarge,* the crew saw the Confederate flag slowly disappear, to be replaced with a white one. Pease's crew had fired the shots that ended the duel. The last well-directed shell had mortally damaged the *Alabama.* She would fight no more.

Negroes at Sea

While the victorious crew cheered, the *Alabama*'s bow rose high above the water. She stood straight up on her end for a second, then disappeared under the water. Pease had performed with such distinction that Acting Master David H. Sumner, his superior officer, personally congratulating the Negro, said, "You sustained your reputation as one of the best men on the ship."

For "marked coolness, good conduct, and qualities even higher than courage and fortitude" Joachim Pease, the determined, likeable New York Negro, became the second man of his race to earn the Navy Medal of Honor.

Men like Pease eventually find themselves in some crisis and react in their own ways. At times they display more courage than they realize they have. Such was the case with twenty-seven-year-old John Lawson, a native of Pennsylvania.

Lawson was a restless sort of an individual. He disliked the rebellion in the South. When the call went out for men to serve in the Union Navy, he was one of the first Pennsylvania Negroes to volunteer. He enlisted as a landsman, the title then bestowed on new, inexperienced sailors.

The short, stocky Negro served aboard the *Hartford,* Rear Admiral David G. Farragut's flagship. His physique made him ideally suited for duty in the relatively crowded shell whip on the berth deck just below the main gun stations. He saw action during the capture of New Orleans, the bombardment of Vicksburg and at Port Hudson.

These were fierce and demanding battles, but Lawson's test of valor was yet to come.

At seven fifty-two on August 5, 1864, the 2,790-ton *Hartford* led a fleet of fourteen Union vessels into Mobile Bay off Alabama. She had just sustained rebel attacks from Forts Gaines, Morgan and Powell. At about eight, out of the smoke and morning haze, appeared the Confederate ship *Tennessee,* moving in for the attack. As the rebels opened fire, the Union ships retaliated; the *Hartford's* nine-inch smooth-bore guns unleashing shells at five-minute intervals.

Below the gun deck, young Lawson and five other men, perspiration running down their faces and bare chests, were busy tugging the shell whip. The whip was made of two-inch rope, rove through two single blocks, extended in a hatchway and was knotted at both ends. Union ships were equipped with this device to raise powder boxes to the gun deck and lower the empty ones, which were then filled by powderboys at the lower deck.

Suddenly, an enemy shell exploded in the midst of the six-man shell whip. Lawson was immediately thrown violently against the bulkhead of the ship. Another landsman, Wilson Brown, a white Natchez, Mississip-

pian, was knocked off the berth deck and fell uncon-
scious through the hatchway to the lower deck. The
remaining three landsmen and an armorer lay lifeless on
the deck, one with a neat round hole, smaller than a
dime, almost exactly between the eyes.

Lawson lay slumped against the side of the ship.
When he tried to get up, he found he couldn't move. His
left leg felt dead. Numb and bewildered, he couldn't
see the limb. "Oh, Lawd," he mumbled. "I don' los'
mah leg."

Then he discovered he was sitting on it. A medic
arrived on the scene. "You're wounded, John," he said.
"Let me take you below."

"No," Lawson said. "Ah reckon 'taint wuth while."

The Negro pulled himself up, trying to shake off the
bewilderment. His left leg was bleeding. Slowly he
looked around and saw his dead comrades. "Lawd," he
said, "de shell whip."

For the first time he felt pain from the shrapnel
wound in his leg. Despite the throbbing, he limped toward his station at the whip. The medic pleaded with
him to have the leg treated, but he refused, saying: "De
guns mus' be surved fust."

For the duration of the duel, which lasted several
hours, Lawson pulled the whip. This was the only means
of supplying the gun crews above. Pain stabbed his leg.
Ignoring the wound and the shell bursts above him, he

faithfully raised and lowered the powder boxes. Though dizzy, he seemed almost disdainful of the danger of falling through the hatchway to the deck below. The important thing was that the gun crews were getting the powder to ward off the rebel attack.

At ten that morning the *Tennessee*'s commander, Captain J. D. Johnston, acknowledged defeat. The victory was a significant one for the Union. Landsman John Lawson had saved the *Hartford,* because he "steadfastly continued his duties" serving the guns, risking death above and beyond the call of duty. Three months later he was awarded the Navy Medal of Honor for his courage.

The last of the four Negroes to receive the Navy Medal of Honor during the Civil War was Aaron Anderson, another Landsman. He served aboard the U. S. S. *Wyandank.*

Anderson was born on a farm in Plymouth, North Carolina. He moved to Philadelphia and enlisted in the Navy on April 17, 1863. When he signed aboard the *Wyandank* he was carried on the rolls as "Sanderson" through an administrative error. The five-foot-nine Negro was a quiet seaman. Yet he was loyal, hardworking and could be depended on to react with prudence in any situation.

During a boat expedition on March 17, 1865, Anderson displayed his ability to think quickly and act accordingly.

The steamship *Wyandank* was on patrol to clear the Mattox Creek in North Carolina of rebel forces. The Confederates were a stubborn and determined force. So many shells were exploding with such surprising force that the Union crew had difficulty returning the fire.

A direct hit exploded on the deck, knocking out a gun crew. Anderson, who was fifty years old at the time, took cover against the onslaught. As he did, another shell slammed into the deck, hurling him through the air. Dazed and bruised, but intact, he shook his head clear and glanced about the deck.

The rebels had shot away half one paddle wheel, pierced her launch in several places and cut away the barrel of a cannon that was being fired against them.

Another shell exploded. It was as though the world was coming apart. Anderson fell to the deck, rolled over on his back and single-handedly loaded the unmanned howitzer. He pounded a wide area—to his front, left and far left—but concentrated on the enemy's main stronghold. He moved so fast and fired so accurately that the force was virtually eliminated.

His daring and fortitude made the creek safe for use by future Union vessels. The citation accompanying his Medal of Honor credited Landsman Aaron Anderson with carrying out "his duties courageously in the face of devastating fire."

It was seven years before any other Negro sailors were acclaimed heroes by their nation. Then, in 1872, two Negroes made their marks in U. S. naval history. They were James H. Conyers and Joseph B. Noil.

Conyers, a native of South Carolina, became the first of his race to enter the U. S. Naval Academy at Annapolis. He was not graduated. Yet his admittance opened the door for the enrollment of Alonzo G. McClellan, another South Carolinian; Henry B. Baker of Mississippi; and other Negroes in the years that followed.

Joseph B. Noil was the first post-Civil War Negro seaman to earn the Navy Medal of Honor. He was a New Yorker of Nova Scotian descent. Noil's action while serving aboard the U. S. S. *Powhatan* on December 26, 1872, is evidence that courage is a quality useful not only in time of war. Thirty-one years old at the time, he saved Boatswain J. C. Walton from drowning while the *Powhatan* was anchored off Norfolk, Virginia.

Seaman Noil earned the medal for his courageous act as did Ship's Cook First Class Daniel Atkins twenty-six years later. Atkins was decorated for risking his life responding to the pleas of two drowning crewmen. It happened off Key West, Florida, on February 11, 1898, shortly before Atkins' thirty-first birthday.

Atkins was born in Brunswick, Virginia, and his only

claim to fame before that fateful February day was his cooking. The crew often raved over his bean soup.

The U. S. S. *Cushing* was heading for Havana, Cuba. The sea was rough. Atkins was in the galley, going about his duties despite the ship's bobbing and weaving. Up on the main deck Ensign Joseph C. Breckenridge was making his way to his quarters.

Suddenly a giant wave swept the deck. In less than a second Breckenridge had disappeared. The force of the wave had knocked him overboard.

"Man overboard, man overboard," someone yelled.

From the railing the victim could be seen struggling to keep his head above water as the waves violently enveloped him. One seaman threw him a lifeline. It was carried out of the ensign's reach by the raging sea.

Lieutenant Albert Gleaves, the *Cushing's* commander, rushed to the scene, saw the struggling officer, then ordered: "Stop engines and put helm to port."

When the engines stopped, John Everetts and Frank Cappage threw two life preservers to Breckenridge. They fell short. Then the lieutenant ordered a starboard lifeboat lowered.

The boat, containing Everetts and Cappage, filled with water the minute it touched the sea. It tipped to one side, and Cappage was swept overboard. Everetts was forced to leave the boat. Both were pulled aboard the *Cushing*, leaving the lifeboat adrift.

Negro Medal of Honor Men

By now Breckenridge's body had been carried about thirty feet from the vessel by the waves. Lieutenant Gleaves ordered that the *Cushing* be advanced closer to the now motionless ensign. It was obvious he was dead. When the engines stopped, Everetts dived from the forecastle with a line that was to be secured around the officer's waist.

Atkins, the Negro cook, appeared on the deck just as Everetts jumped. He watched calmly as the gunner's mate from Theroid, Canada, struggled to reach Breckenridge's lifeless body.

A giant wave overpowered Everetts, causing him to panic. Others on the deck stood horrified, but not Atkins. He hurriedly took off his shoes and outer garments, grabbed a lifeline, climbed the railing and jumped into the choppy sea. Atkins wasn't an experienced swimmer, but he had courage.

While the rest of the crew, standing safely shoulder to shoulder along the rail on the deck, selfishly content with their situations, looked on, iron-nerved Atkins was risking death to rescue two white companions.

He reached Everetts and Breckenridge just as they were being separated. The sea was cold and fought Atkins' every rescue attempt. As if that weren't enough, Everetts was struggling, fighting and kicking. For the first time Atkins felt fear.

The wave that engulfed him and his companions was

like a blow in the face. He ached all over, but managed to grab the gunner's mate's lifeline, then Brecken-ridge's. One by one, Breckenridge, Everetts, then Atkins, were pulled aboard the *Cushing*.

Atkins had displayed the courage and determination many men envy. He earned the Navy Medal of Honor for "gallant conduct and courage."

Robert Penn was the only Negro seaman during the Spanish-American War period to receive the Navy Medal of Honor. He was born in City Point, Virginia, just seven years after the Civil War had ended. As a boy, he worked in the fields and received very little education. Not satisfied with his existence, he enlisted in the Navy for what he called "a better life." Sea duty was good for Penn. He learned much from traveling and gained self-confidence after experiencing racial humiliation in his home town. By early 1898 he had progressed to Fireman Second Class.

Penn was proud of his accomplishments, but he never considered himself a courageous man.

Yet this latent attribute came to the surface on July 20, 1898. Penn was just three months from his twenty-sixth birthday and serving aboard the U. S. S. *Iowa*. He was stationed in a compartment next to Boiler Room Number Two. It was early morning. The *Iowa* was anchored off Santiago de Cuba.

Shortly before seven there was an explosion in the

boiler room. By instinct, Fireman Second Class Penn rushed to the scene. He stopped short at the door.

It was a frightening sight. A manhole gasket had blown off one of the boilers, releasing one hundred twenty pounds of pressure. The room was quickly being filled with steam. Boiling water covered the floor.

He turned to get help, but through the haze he saw a figure move. Instantly, he entered the room, despite the scalding water, just in time to save the injured coal passer from falling. Penn was medium-built, but he managed to carry the muscular, one-hundred-forty-pound man over his shoulders to safety. The coal passer had both feet scalded and a deep gash on his forehead. Penn's clothes clung to his ebony skin from the steam. His shoes seemed heavy as lead after walking through the hot water.

While the passer was being treated for his wounds, Penn returned to the boiler room. The fire, which had now begun to seep out of the furnace, could have caused another explosion, but the Negro fearlessly disregarded that danger. He built a bridge by throwing a plank across two ash buckets. The board rested just one foot above the boiling water.

Onlookers like Assistant Engineer Stuckney and Fireman Smith watched spellbound as Penn cautiously matched wits with the odds. Slowly, inch by inch, he crept sideways on the board, carrying shovels of flaming coals from the furnace to a safe place.

The board sagged in the middle from Penn's weight. Despite this he continued to brave the blinding steam, heat and smoke, making his way from the furnace to another part of the room. During each trip vapor from the boiling water on the floor enveloped him, impairing his vision as he risked scalding to prevent another explosion.

When the last coals were removed there was a thunderous sigh of relief. Young Penn, bewildered at what he had done, leaned against a bulkhead as the crew praised his courage. The Negro, by his fearlessness and quickness had averted an explosion that could have destroyed the *Iowa* and taken the lives of many of its crew.

On December 14, four months and six days after that display of courage, Fireman Second Class Robert Penn, the former field hand from City Point, Virginia, was awarded the Navy Medal of Honor for intrepidity at the risk of his own life above and beyond the call of duty.

When Commodore Perry cited the Negro seaman as "insensible to danger," he was in a sense wrong. Courage is not a reckless indifference to death and danger. Regardless of his situation or the color of a man's skin, there are those who do what they feel is right despite the sacrifices.

Negro Medal of Honor Men

While Navy Medal of Honor recipient Joseph B. Noil was risking his life in 1872 to save a fellow crewman, other men of his race were making sacrifices to pave the way for settlement of America's virgin lands. They had death-defying encounters with hostile Indians who roamed the plains.

★

CHAPTER V

★

The Indian Fighters

SEPTEMBER 17, 1891 was a clear day at Fort Robinson, Nebraska. In front of the post headquarters building a formation of soldiers stood rigidly at attention. The relative quiet was broken as a young officer read a citation: ". . . Such an example of soldierlike conduct is worthy of imitation and reflects credit. . . ."

Seconds later a general walked up to one of the soldiers and pinned on him the nation's most coveted military award—the Medal of Honor. The enlisted man was Sergeant William O. Wilson, a Negro and native of Hagerstown, Maryland. He had earned the decoration eight months before in a fight with hostile Sioux Indians.

Of the 419 Medals of Honor awarded during the Indian campaigns, 13 were received by Negroes. But if it had been left up to some citizens the colored soldier would not have been able to earn the distinction.

After the Civil War a quiet debate erupted on what to do with Negroes who wanted to continue military service. Some civic leaders were against making them a part of the Regular Army. Others, like historian Edward L. N. Glass, favored maintaining the black patriots. Realizing the Negroes' value on Civil War battlefields, Glass said:

> As soldiers the colored men compare favorably with white men. . . . They manifest a remarkable aptitude and desire for acquiring knowledge whenever opportunities have been afforded them. As to bodily strength and natural physique, they are not inferior, and in some respects, they are superior as the records of the War Department will show. They are more temperate in habit, more readily disciplined, and take greater pride in performance of military duty. As a rule they are better fitted for soldiers than white men.

Reflections like these were instrumental in the creation of a career force of all-Negro units. Congress, in the reorganization act of 1866, authorized the establishment of four regiments of colored enlisted men. They became the Ninth and Tenth Cavalry and Twenty-fourth and Twenty-fifth Infantry. White officers took command of the ranks as their first assignment after graduating from the U. S. Military Academy at West Point, New York.

The Ninth Cavalry was organized in New Orleans,

The Indian Fighters

Louisiana, during the winter of 1866–67. From 1867 to 1890 the unit was constantly in the field fighting hostile Indians. The most important of its encounters were with the Sioux during the winter of 1890–91. As Historian Theophilus Gould Steward pointed out, "The regiment was first in the field in November and the last to leave, late that following March." The weather was severe that winter, but from Fort Robinson, Nebraska, and Fort Cummings, New Mexico, the Negro Indian fighters earned their share of victories even before the Sioux Campaign.

Unlike the black patriots of Civil War fame, men of the Ninth and Tenth did not march gallantly into battle with drums rolling, bugles blowing and flags flying. They patrolled a strange, desolate country occupied by hostile Indians whose manner of warfare was always unorthodox. The ambush became an everyday incident; but they learned to ride shadowed by the hills and with the ease with which most men cross a quiet street.

The Apaches were the first adversaries of the Army. Their warriors were bloodthirsty. Kill for the sake of killing was their motive as they roamed the deserts in search of the white man.

Sergeant Emanuel Stance was the first Negro Indian fighter to earn the Medal of Honor. He was a member of Company F, Ninth United States Cavalry, Fort Mc-Kavett, Texas, at the time.

Negro Medal of Honor Men

On May 20, 1870, Captain Henry Carroll, Sergeant Stance and a detachment of nine men left the fort on a routine patrol. Just fourteen miles from their station, traveling along Kickapoo Road, they discovered a band of Indians riding up a hill with a small herd of horses. The cavalrymen pursued the renegades and became involved in a mild skirmish. Outnumbered, the Indians disappeared behind some mountains, leaving the nine horses, which were taken by the soldiers.

It was getting dark, so the captain ordered his men to make overnight camp near Kickapoo Springs. At six the next morning they broke camp and headed for the fort. Ten miles from Kickapoo they spotted about twenty Indians who were pursuing a couple of herds of government horses. They greatly outnumbered the guards accompanying the animals. Captain Carroll ordered the attack. For eight miles there was a running fight. Sergeant Stance, who had had about five encounters similar to this one in the past two years, led the left flank. Far ahead of his men he rode, shooting and yelling for them to press the attack. Soon the Indians were out of sight. The fight had ended as quickly as it had begun. On May 21, the detachment rode into Fort McKavett with twenty-five horses taken during the two-day patrol.

Sergeant Stance was commended by Captain Carroll for his courage and devotion and was recommended for the Medal of Honor. He received the coveted award on

The Indian Fighters

July 24, 1870. In a letter to the Adjutant General in Washington, D.C., Stance wrote, "I will cherish the gift as a thing of priceless value and endeavor by my future conduct to merit the high honor confirmed upon me."

In that year James W. Smith of South Carolina became the first Negro to enter the U. S. Military Academy. He did not graduate, but instead left and became supervisor of cadets at what is now known as South Carolina State College. Henry O. Flipper, seven years later, was the first of his race to graduate from West Point. The Thomasville, Georgia, Negro's initial assignment was with the Tenth Cavalry.

While Lieutenant Flipper was becoming acclimated to his new career, Corporal Clinton Greaves was on his third patrol with Company C, Ninth Cavalry. It was June 24, 1877. Lieutenant Henry H. Wright, five Negro soldiers and three Navajo scouts were riding through New Mexico's Florida Mountains. Their destination was the San Carlos reservation. The detachment had been ordered to relieve forty or fifty Chiricahua Indians of their weapons and horses.

The tribe was at peace with the white man. The lieutenant did not want to risk an uprising by using force, so he called a council with the tribal chiefs. For thirty minutes the young officer tried to reason with the Indians. They refused to give up their rifles and horses, saying that without them there would be no defense if the white man did not keep his word. While the pow-wow dragged on, eighteen armed Apache bucks had surrounded the reservation. A sharp crackle of rifle fire electrified the soldiers. The shots sent them scrambling for what little protection there was in the open spaces. Chiricahua women and children ran for their tepees.

In the fight that followed Corporal Greaves coura-geously engaged in hand-to-hand combat with a group of the attackers. The five-foot-seven-inch, 165-pound na-tive of Madison County, Virginia, defiantly erect at one point, killed one of the warriors. The rest, obviously surprised at his boldness, retreated to surrounding cliffs and rocks. From there they directed concentrated at-tacks, firing and yelling with all their energy.

The Indians had a strategic advantage over the sol-diers. Rocks and cliffs provided them with protection the lieutenant's men did not have on level ground. The situation grew more serious with every shot. The caval-rymen were running short of ammunition, several men had been killed or wounded. "Withdraw, withdraw," the officer ordered. Greaves took the initiative. He crouched as close to the ground as possible, with bullets falling about him, and moved toward the horses. Dirt flew as the pellets hit the ground, but he managed to rescue three horses. Later, with rarely equaled accu-racy, he shot two Indians through the top of their heads as they glanced above the rocks. In desperation the detachment finally retreated to Fort Cummings with eleven horses and a few rifles. For his daring the corporal was awarded the Medal of Honor on June 26, 1879.

This was the year Apache chief Victorio decided to fight rather than have his people confined to reservations. With a force of more than a hundred warriors he began a series of the most baffling movements the Army ever encountered during the Indian campaigns. Victorio was a perfect master of deception, leaving trails of blood, death and destruction as he evaded the cavalrymen.

The Ninth played key roles in the pursuit of Victorio. During this bloody game of tag two Negroes—Sergeants Thomas Boyne and John Denny—earned Medals of Honor for gallantry and intrepidity in action.

Boyne, born in Prince Georges County, Maryland, earned the award for bravery in two encounters. The first was on May 29, 1879. Lieutenant Henry H. Wright (the same officer who was with Corporal Greaves at the San Carlos reservation) was on his way to Fort Stanton with a wounded soldier. Assisting and providing protection in this humanitarian effort was a detachment led by Sergeant Boyne.

Cautiously they rode, their horses struggling through the Membres Mountains of New Mexico. Boyne knew the mountains well. He was also familiar with the cunning tactics of Victorio's band. They had matched wits against the best in the Army and won many skirmishes. As the soldiers approached a series of ridges they were met by a war whoop and a volley of rifle shots.

"Victorio," someone yelled. The detachment scattered, but not Boyne. He flanked the Indian warriors, then gallantly charged them, firing with such precision and rapidity that they were driven off. With yells sounding sharp and clear above the thunder of galloping horses, the small band of Indians disappeared in a smother of dust over the hills.

In the months that followed the troops groped frantically through the desert for the Apaches, but Victorio's people were gone almost as if they had disappeared into the air. Finally, on September 18, the Ninth Cavalry thought they had the desert wolves trapped.

Lieutenant Colonel N. A. M. Dudley and Captain Charles D. Beyers led four companies of Negroes that seemed to have the Indians immobilized in the canyons at the head of Las Animas Creek. The Apaches were badly outnumbered, but in spite of this they could not be driven from impregnable positions among the rocks.

Throughout the day the constant crack of rifle fire echoed through the hills and canyons. From bush to bush, rock to rock the enemy appeared, then disappeared, taking their toll of Dudley's men. The Indians had killed five enlisted men, two Navajo scouts and one

The Indian Fighters

white civilian scout, wounded many soldiers and killed or crippled thirty-eight horses. On assessing the situation, Dudley decided that Victorio's men were too strong.

As darkness began to fall, Captain Beyers ordered a retreat. "We'll move out when it gets dark, firing three volleys from our guns as we leave," he instructed. First the cavalrymen had to gather the wounded. There was the danger of being shot in the rescues, yet all but one man was saved. He was Private Freeland, who had been shot in the leg while trying to advance closer to the Indians. There he lay in agony on a rock crest hill about four hundred yards from the soldiers' positions. Freeland, supported by a comrade, tried to walk on one leg but was unable to make it. The ground was rocky, and the Indians hampered the attempt with constant rifle shots.

During a lull in the fighting Sergeant Denny looked over the crest. Freeland was there, painfully pulling himself along with his hands, inch by inch, toward his comrades.

The sight of that man dragging himself helplessly was too much for Denny. He leaped over the crest. "No, John," someone yelled. Ignoring the plea, the sergeant jumped up and dashed for the wounded man. He bent double to present as small a target as possible along the three-hundred-yard stretch. Bullets were singing in his ears, but he unflinchingly reached his destination. The private was larger, but he climbed on the sergeant's back and was carried to safety behind a rock.

The withdrawal began. Orange flashes spurted out in the darkness as the cavalrymen, carrying their dead and wounded, fired three volleys from rifles as planned. Returning to Fort Stanton the Negro sergeant's superior officer, Lieutenant Matthias W. Day, described the rescue as "an act of most conspicuous gallantry." The Big Flats, New York, hero was stationed at Fort Robinson fifteen years later. It was there that he received the Medal of Honor.

Nine days after Denny's courageous act, Sergeant Boyne had his second heroic encounter with Victorio's forces. On September 27 Major Albert P. Morrow, with more than a hundred officers and enlisted men of the Ninth Cavalry, clashed with the warrior near Ojo Caliente, New Mexico. For two days the Indians and cavalrymen fought a running battle. Sergeant Boyne's conspicuous bravery during the fight was justification enough for him to wear the Medal of Honor three years later. He killed one of three warriors incapacitated and single-handedly captured a considerable number of the sixty horses and mules taken.

Meanwhile, also in late September, 1879, other elements of the U. S. Cavalry were engaged in combating the terrorist activities of another tribe—the Utes. Major

The Indian Fighters

T. T. Thornburgh, with three hundred white cavalrymen and a company of one hundred and fifty infantrymen, left Fort Steele, Colorado, in pursuit of the
renegades. They were riding cautiously through Red
Canyon. Suddenly, with a series of wild yells, the
drum roll of a rifle volley and blankets waving, a group
of Ute raiders broke out of an adjacent gorge.

The white cavalrymen took defensive positions. The
Indians scattered, took cover in the cedar and piñon
brush and rocks that covered the hills on each side of
the narrow valley. Over the barren desert near Milk
River the soldiers dug in for the fight.

The Indians held the soldiers pinned down for two
days. The longer they fought it out, the greater their
chances were of not returning to Fort Steele. Troops
were running out of ammunition. Most of their horses
had been killed, and fifty-six men, more than 40 per cent
of the command, lay dead or wounded. Among them
were the lifeless bodies of Major Thornburgh and the
company surgeon. Captain Payne, now in command,
called for volunteers to carry a message for help. Private Edward F. Murphy, a wiry, hard-riding Irishman,
was chosen. He mounted one of the few unwounded
horses and rode hard.

Throughout the day the fight continued. Then shortly
after sunrise on October 2 the sound of galloping hoofs
was heard down the valley. There were shots and cheers

as Captain Francis S. Dodge led elements of the Negro Ninth Cavalry through the canyon. "Private Murphy got through," the officer announced as he made his appearance, "and more help is on the way."

The arrival of reinforcements did not deter the Utes. From the surrounding hills sniping continued. But in typical fashion not an Indian was in sight. There would be a puff of smoke. When a soldier returned the shot, his foe was usually yards away behind another boulder or bush. Soon the horses of the Negro soldiers, like those of their white comrades, were dead or wounded. Dodge and his men dug their elbows into the dirt with the other soldiers and settled down to the siege.

The captain brought with him rugged, twenty-one-year-old Sergeant Henry Johnson, who earned the Medal of Honor during this engagement. He had enlisted in the cavalry at Baltimore, Maryland, just one year and ten months before accompanying Dodge's rescue party that October second. Johnson's superiors considered him capable of sound judgment and highly qualified for handling men. For this reason he served as Sergeant of the Guard for the Ninth's D Company.

It was in this capacity that the Negro was serving during the Milk River siege. His principal assignment was to issue instructions to sentries guarding the Army's wagons and supplies. Defying repeated attempts by the Indians to hamper this assignment, the Boynton, Virginia-born Negro went from sentry post to sentry post urging his men to stay alert. "Fire on any movin' brush and aim for the top of thar heads when they rise behind boulders to shoot," he instructed the soldiers. When darkness came, with it evolved a new peril—the enemy might attack during the night. Johnson worked to guarantee the sentinels' alertness. His efforts for two nights were in vain, for the shrewd Utes wasted no ammunition in the darkness.

During the day, while the night sentries tried to sleep at the breastworks, Sergeant Johnson aided the suffering wounded. They were begging for water. Some men volunteered to crawl down to the river and fill canteens. But shots from Indian positions drove them back. Johnson saw the attempts and became concerned. He volunteered to take the risk. As riflemen covered him he cautiously crawled down the bank. From two ridges the keen-eyed Indian marksmen took pot shots at the Negro; each bullet barely missed its mark. But he continued to take chances, filling canteens, then moving from ono wounded comrade—white or colored—to the other with water.

Two days after Johnson's God-sent arrival at Milk River, General Wesley Merrit arrived from Fort Russell with four troops of cavalry and a company of infantry. The fighting continued sporadically the following morning. About 11 A.M. the general prepared his men for an assault on the Ute positions, but by noon the warriors had slipped away.

When the soldiers returned to their post Sergeant Johnson's superiors were loud in praising his conduct during the battle. On recommending him for the Medal of Honor they cited "his courage, devotion to duty and humanitarian action at Milk River."

This was one of the last battles with the Utes. They soon retreated to reservations in Utah and southern Colorado. In four months another Negro, this one from Williamson County, Tennessee, also earned a place on the Medal of Honor roll. He was Sergeant George Jordan, a five-foot-six rifleman with a sure finger and keen eyesight. On May 14, 1880, with fourteen years of military service behind him, he had his first confrontation with Chief Victorio, the "Apache Wolf."

Sergeant Jordan was commanding a detachment of twenty-five men at Fort Tulerso, New Mexico. A party of one hundred Indians attacked the outpost. Demonstrating courage, leadership and keen marksmanship, Jordan led the fight in repulsing the renegades. On August 12, 1881, he prevented his command from being surrounded and wiped out by Apaches. This time, with nineteen men, he stubbornly held his ground in the rocks of Carrizo Canyon and gallantly forced the Indians back.

Sergeants Johnson and Jordan received their Medals

of Honor at Fort Robinson, Nebraska, in 1890. Chief Victorio died months later in a fight with Mexican soldiers. Jordan, the heroic patriot of Fort Tulerso and Carrizo Canyon, retired from military service on April 5, 1897, at the age of forty-nine. He spent the rest of his life on a pension of twelve dollars per month in Washington, D.C. at the U. S. Soldiers Home.

Victorio's death by no means ended the skirmishes between Negro Indian fighters and their foe. Chief Nana, a friend of the Apache Wolf, took over where his comrade left off. It took him more than a half year to prepare for battle, but by July, 1881, the short, fat and wrinkled eighty-year-old man was ready. So were the black patriots. They dogged Nana through Alamo Canyon, over the San Andreas Mountains and La Savoya Desert.

On August 16, 1881, Nana's warriors and the Negro cavalrymen clashed in the Cuchillo Negro Mountains of New Mexico. Three Medals of Honor were earned during this confrontation.

Company I, Ninth Cavalry was camped at Canada Alamosa, New Mexico, when at about noon word came that Indians had attacked Chaney Ranch about two miles away. The band had murdered the husband, wife, two children and two sheepherders. Second Lieutenant George R. Burnett, the company's white commander,

71

ordered his troops to saddle up, then led a detachment of Negro and Mexican soldiers to the scene.

The Indians were disguised as Mexicans, wearing blankets over their shoulders and sombreros. As the lieutenant and his men approached from a distance, one of the warriors beckoned for them to come closer. The cavalrymen spurred their horses and hastily advanced toward what they thought were friendly forces. Within one thousand feet the Indians opened fire and then withdrew. Immediately, First Sergeant Moses Williams, leading the right flank, and the Mexicans, on the left, pursued the now retreating Indians.

After a few miles, during the running battle, Sergeant Williams stopped to signal Lieutenant Burnett to come ahead. But in the initial contact Burnett's horse had run away. He was thus cut off from the main force of his troops. Beside him stood Private Augustus Walley, providing protection for the officer. Williams rode back to the pair, but Lieutenant Burnett ordered him to go look for another group of cavalrymen to assist his company.

The sergeant met Lieutenant Gustavus Valois and his men a short distance away. The officer and his men, Williams leading them, rode through Cuchillo Negro Mountains in search of the Indians. Always from cover, with never a sign of where they lurked, Nana's braves snaked through the mesquite and cactus until they were in good positions for the attack. About one hundred fifty yards from the renegades' positions, Williams saw one of them move. "Injuns," he warned the soldiers. The cavalrymen dispersed just as rifles opened fire on them from the hills above. The canyon rang with war whoops and rifle bursts. Courageously, with precision calm, the soldiers aimed over rocks, pulling their triggers every time an Indian appeared long enough for a good shot. In spite of their efforts Nana's men were too much for the cavalrymen.

The fighting was fierce. With determined accuracy the Indians picked off soldier after soldier; a good share of the horses were dead or crippled by the Apaches. Lieutenant Valois, fearing that the detachment would be wiped out, ordered his men to fall back and take other positions. As the men retreated Private Burton's reddish-brown bay balked, then galloped toward the enemy's positions with its rider. The soldier jumped out of his saddle, landing about a hundred yards from the Apaches. Walley and Lieutenant Burnett witnessed the incident and presumed the man had been shot. A short distance from him lay Privates Glasby and Wilson. Their horses had been killed, and they could not escape because of a devastating crossfire.

By now Sergeant Williams, who had escorted Lieutenant Valois through the mountains, had returned to the place where Burnett and Walley were trapped. The lieutenant, in his report of the incident, said the two

Negroes were "always by my side in every danger." Just as they prepared to fall back and take other positions they heard a plea from behind a prairie dog mound about two hundred yards away.

"Please, Lieutenant, for God's sake don't leave us. Our lives depend on you."

"Who's there," the lieutenant asked.

"Privates Burton, Glasby and Wilson, suh," was the reply.

"Burton!" the officer exclaimed, looking at Williams and Walley. "I thought he was shot when his horse ran away."

"I order you to come out of there and keep low," the officer yelled.

Glasby and Wilson crawled out and made their way to the cavalrymen's position. "Where's Burton?" Sergeant Williams asked.

"He can't come out, Sarge, I think he's hurt."

"Private Walley," the officer said, "try to get that man out of there."

The next few minutes would prove to be the greatest challenge of the Reisterstown, Maryland, Negro's short military career. He mounted his horse and rode low in the saddle, defying a hail of bullets from the enemy as he made his way to Burton. Arriving at the stranded soldier's side, Walley quickly dismounted, helped Burton into the saddle, mounted again. Then the two rode back to the cavalry's lines. Bullets whizzed by them as they made their getaway. Williams meanwhile had fired on Indian positions to keep them from hampering the escape. Wilson and Glasby lay horrified as the two ended their death-defying journey. "It is a source of mystery to me how they escaped unhurt, considering the short range," Lieutenant Burnett said later.

Suddenly, from the direction where the trio had been rescued, another fight broke out. This was with Private Martin, another of Lieutenant Valois' men, who had also lost his horse and was caught behind enemy lines. When Lieutenant Burnett looked up the Indians were surrounding the lone soldier. The young white officer from Lower Providence Township, Pennsylvania, mounted his horse and galloped to the Negro private's assistance. His horse was shot in the rescue, but in spite of threatening bullets he held off the Indian attacks with a six-shooter and returned with Martin to safety.

Later Nana, satisfied that he had left the detachment so it could not follow him, withdrew as quickly as he had gone into action. A small force led by fresh reinforcements tried to stop the warriors by flanking them, but the effort failed.

Lieutenant Burnett, Sergeant Williams and Private Walley, all of whom performed heroically during the four-hour engagement, earned Medals of Honor for their steadfastness and courage.

Negro Medal of Honor Men

Company B of the Ninth Cavalry also made contact with Chief Nana and his renegades three days later. It was hot that August 19, 1881. Lieutenant George W. Smith was leading twenty colored cavalrymen and a group of civilians when they were confronted with the Indians in New Mexico's Gaballan Canyon. The civilians were cowboys who, the day before, joined the company to help the soldiers and see the fun. The combined force outnumbered Nana's warriors. Yet the odds failed to worry the defiant Apache. He chose his ground, and the dusty Indians took cover. The drifting smoke and staccato rattle of their rifles dominated ridges just above the party.

The Apache fire was wicked and deadly. George Daly, the cowboys' leader, was killed almost instantly. Here and there the colored soldiers dropped as the bullets found their marks. Lieutenant Smith, while directing his men to positions, crumpled dead in the sagebrush.

The young officer's death for a time demoralized the men. They were left without a leader. Sergeant Edward L. Baker, Jr., who seventeen years later won the Medal of Honor for bravery at Santiago, Cuba, was the company's next senior man. But for some reason he was not present, so Sergeant Brent Woods of Pulaski, Kentucky, took command.

He had only two years, seven months as a cavalryman,

The Indian Fighters

but the Negro Kentuckian carried out his responsibilities like a seasoned combat veteran. Woods, displaying energy and skill, rallied his men, then led the civilians to safety behind a boulder. Afterward he directed a charge against the enemy on one side of the canyon. In advance of his men, the spirited Negro fought his way to a high ridge. From there he conducted a one-man war on the Indians, eventually driving them from their positions. A small force of Apaches tried to attack Woods from the right. A bullet grazed his arm, but he held his ground and shot with such accuracy and speed that they stopped their advance. The retaliation was so devastating the warriors left their positions, mounted horses and rode away.

The fight was over. Six men were dead, and others, including Sergeant Woods, were wounded. One of the white cowboys saved by the valiant Negro later said, "That Sergeant Woods is an s.o.b. to fight. I had no idea a darky would fight that way. If it had not been for him none of us would have come out of that canyon."

About ten months after this daring skirmish in Gaballan Canyon, Chief Nana surrendered. In one of the last campaigns to deter the old warrior's murderous activities, Sergeant Woods had earned the Medal of Honor for conspicuous gallantry and intrepidity.

Indians were not the only threat to settlers of the

Negro Medal of Honor Men

Southwest. Robbers often roamed the desert and plains in search of unsuspecting and defenseless travelers. On some occasions even the presence of troops failed to deter their murderous raids. Such was the case with a military wagon train traveling in Arizona in mid-1889.

It was on May 11. Two wagons left Fort Grant to deliver the April payroll to troops at Fort Thomas. The money wagon contained $29,000. Accompanying the cash was Major J. W. Wham, paymaster; W. T. Gibbon, his clerk; a Negro servant; and eleven soldiers of the all-Negro Twenty-fourth U. S. Cavalry, who served as escorts. They carried revolvers and carbines. Sergeant Benjamin Brown and Corporal Isaiah Mays, both Virginians, were the ranking enlisted men.

Shortly after noon that day the party arrived at a hill crest between Cedar Springs and Fort Thomas. As they reached the crest, Sergeant Brown signaled the group to halt. Major Wham yelled: "What's the matter, Sergeant?"

"A boulder in the road, suh," replied Brown.

By now all the troops had dismounted and formed a security perimeter around the wagon train. One of the privates moved from the escort to the money wagon; a corporal, Mays, stayed with the payroll carrier.

"All men except those guarding the wagons, come help me move this boulder," Sergeant Brown ordered. Just as the group assembled near the rock a voice called

78

Army Medal of Honor

Navy and Marine Corps Medal of Honor

Air Force Medal of Honor

Lieutenant General Benjamin O. Davis, Jr., the first Negro to attain three-star rank in U. S. military history

Company E, Fourth U. S. Colored Troops at Fort Lincoln

Band of the 107th U. S. Colored Troops of the Civil War

U. S. Colored Troops after a mine disaster at Petersburg, Virginia

Courtesy U. S. Air Force

Captains Leonard Saunders and Ross Randolph in a Minuteman intercontinental
ballistics missile launch center

Vietnam War Medal of Honor winner Private First Class Milton
L. Olive III of Chicago, Illinois

from atop a ledge on the east side of the road. "Hold up your hands!" (Or "Let that rock alone!" or "Run, you black s.o.b.!" Postmaster Wham in his War Department report could not remember just what was said.) The sounds were followed by a shot, then a volley from the ridge.

The first man hit was Private Lewis, the money-wagon driver. He fell from his seat with a wound in the stomach. The mules—twelve of them—bolted, pulling their wagons with them. Two of the animals attached to the money wagon were killed, bringing the carrier to a stop. The escort vehicle had also been halted.

By now a devastating fight was taking place. The badmen were taking their toll of Major Wham's force. Gibbon, the clerk, was wounded. Then one by one the escorts fell; some with only slight wounds. Corporal Mays positioned himself near the escort wagon. When the shooting became heavy he went underneath it, firing four shots, then reloading his carbine. Later he moved to Major Wham's side near the money wagon.

Sergeant Brown was caught in the open during the attack. Near him lay several of his wounded privates, most of whom were unable to fight. Just as he was taking aim with his revolver a bullet entered his abdomen. He fell to the ground, grabbed one of his wounded men's rifles and continued to fight until shot in the arm.

Nearly all of Major Wham's force was by now disabled. The robbers left their positions on the ridge and descended on the soldiers. The paymaster estimated the highwaymen to be fifteen or twenty in number, so he and the remainder of his group retreated to a dry creek bed, leaving the money wagon unattended. Corporal Mays, however, decided to seek help. He crawled and walked two miles to Cottonwood Ranch and asked Barney Norton for assistance. But aid arrived too late. The robbers had broken open the wooden strongbox and made off with the money.

In his final report to the War Department, Major Wham said, ". . . I never witnessed better courage or better fighting than shown by these colored soldiers." Several of Wham's escorts were recommended for the Certificate of Merit for their dedication. But Sergeant Brown and Corporal Mays received the big one. They were awarded the Medal of Honor for courage and gallantry in the confrontation with the robbers.

By early 1890 the Ninth Cavalry had had its share of conflicts with warring Indian tribes. It had also produced a generous number of heroes. But its sister unit, the Tenth Cavalry, was also playing a bloody game of tag with the enemy. They fought their share of battles, losing blood and sweat on the desert during each engagement. In the twenty-year fight with Indians only one enlisted man of the Negro Tenth earned the Medal of Honor. He was Sergeant William McBryar of Elizabethtown, North Carolina. He enlisted at New York City on January 3, 1887.

Company K, Tenth Cavalry had left Fort Thomas, Arizona, on March 7, 1890, in search of the last of a tribe of renegade Apaches. In typical fashion the Indians attacked the patrol as it entered a canyon. Sergeant McBryar earned the Medal of Honor in this fight. First Lieutenant J. W. Watson, in nominating the Negro for the award, said, "Sergeant McBryar demonstrated coolness, bravery, and good marksmanship under circumstances very different from those on the target range." That skirmish was one of the last of the Apache campaign, which closed ten days after McBryar's marksmanship earned for him the coveted decoration.

The Negro Indian fighters now turned their attention to another warring tribe—the Sioux. This band fought differently from the Apaches. They instigated their battles on the plains rather than the desert. Glory was the motive for their killing.

Throughout 1890 the cavalry challenged Sioux chiefs like Sitting Bull, Catch-the-Bear, Jumping Bull and Big Foot. It was in a fight with the latter that Corporal William O. Wilson risked his life to save elements of the Ninth Cavalry from being slaughtered.

On the morning of December thirtieth, a wagon train carrying military supplies and equipment left Pine Ridge Agency, South Dakota. Providing escort were a detachment of colored soldiers and two Indian scouts. When the party reached White Clay Creek near the Cheyenne River, they were attacked by Big Foot's warriors. Again the cavalrymen were outnumbered. From a ridge several yards to the west they began the attack. The troops dismounted and scrambled for cover, some falling prone near the river bank, others under and around the wagons. Sioux warriors were yelling and shooting. The hoof beats of their horses kicked up the dust as they descended on the soldiers. Around them they galloped with war whoops and deadly rifle shots.

The braves were taking their toll of soldiers and horses. The detachment commander, realizing that only reinforcements could save his men, searched for a messenger. He asked the two scouts to take an order for more troops. They refused. "Anyone willing to get help from the agency?" he yelled in desperation.

"Yas, suh," a voice replied a few yards away.

Making his way to the officer, as close to the ground as possible, was Corporal Wilson. "You realize those warriors will try to intercept the message and kill you, soldier," the commander warned.

"I can do it," he replied. Confident that the corporal had the courage to carry out the daring mission to Pine Ridge, the officer hastily scribbled a message and signed it.

The Negro stuffed the paper into his blouse, mounted

The Indian Fighters

a horse and rode for his life. Four Indians bolted after him, shooting and yelling as they rode. One tried to head Wilson off, but it was too late. Bullets fell about the corporal, but he managed to lengthen the distance between him and the enemy.

Nearly an hour had passed before a relief force of fresh soldiers, guns blazing, charged the Indians. They withdrew as the cavalrymen gave pursuit. Corporal Wilson had accomplished his mission. In doing so he became the last Negro to earn the Medal of Honor during the Indian campaigns.

Relative peace eventually came to the desert and plains. The colored cavalrymen had done their part in opening the Southwest. They had fought and died clearing the way for settlement and development of the blood-soaked virgin lands.

In the meantime, trouble was brewing in the Caribbean. Cubans and Spaniards were at odds with each other. To liberate Cuba, the United States sent troops to that country. It was here that the Negro Tenth Cavalry had its days of glory.

★

Salvation at Santiago

Edward L. Baker, Jr. was a personable sergeant major who, like many Negro cavalrymen, transferred to the Tenth U. S. Cavalry from the Ninth after the Indian Campaigns. He earned the Medal of Honor for bravery during the Santiago Campaign of the Spanish-American War.

Baker was born to pioneer parents in a freight wagon on December 28, 1865, near North Platte River, Laramie County, Wyoming. His father was French, his mother mulatto. In 1882 he rejoined the Ninth as a trumpeter. During five years' service with that unit he fought briefly in Gaballan Canyon, New Mexico, on August 19, 1881. It was here that Sergeant Brent Woods earned the Medal of Honor during a fight with Apache Indians.

In 1887 Baker enlisted in the Tenth and in five years

advanced from private to sergeant major. He was constantly seeking ways to improve his military career. He spoke Spanish fluently and had some knowledge of Russian, Chinese and French. Shortly before the Spanish-American War the five-foot-nine Negro applied for an extended furlough in order to attend a cavalry school at Saumur, France. He agreed to pay his own expenses for the opportunity. His application was enthusiastically endorsed by his white superiors. They knew him as an exceptional soldier, and he was highly respected. Baker was, however, unable to attend the school, because before final action was taken on his request the Tenth was ordered to take part in the invasion of Cuba.

Alerted also for duty in Cuba were the Ninth Cavalry and the Twenty-fourth and Twenty-fifth Infantry. They were accompanied by two white battalions of the First Volunteer Cavalry, better known as the Rough Riders. One of the officers in the force was Lieutenant Colonel Theodore Roosevelt, a former Assistant Secretary of the Navy, who later became President of the United States.

The Twenty-fourth and Twenty-fifth Infantry and Ninth and Tenth Cavalry units remained the only all-Negro military organizations authorized for retention in the Regular Army after the Civil War. Their elements were still largely commanded by young white West Point graduates who had little or no combat experience. The Tenth was organized on July 28, 1866, under the same law and at the same time as the Ninth. Fort Leavenworth, Kansas, was its first home. From there the unit launched attacks that were the backbone of the Geronimo campaign force. It succeeded in capturing the wiry Indian warrior in 1885. The Tenth was stationed in the Southwest until 1893, when it moved to Montana. It remained there until the beginning of the Spanish-American War.

The employment of Negro soldiers in Cuba was decided on not merely because they were combat-ready. The insurrection in that country had racial as well as economic overtones. Native Cubans, with a strong infusion of Negro blood, did most of the labor, while the upper-class whites grew rich. Even during economic prosperity the ordinary Cuban, who was just a hair from being a slave, grew discontent with Spanish rule and rebelled. Spanish policy discriminated not only in favor of Spain, but also in favor of a handful of pure-blood Spaniards in Cuba.

These irregularities, plus the brutal treatment ordered by Valeriano Weyler, Spanish commander in Cuba, made life almost unbearable for the Cubans. When the American people heard lurid tales of conditions on the island they demanded action. On April 17, 1898, Congress passed a joint resolution demanding that Spain withdraw from Cuba. The act went on to say that the people of the island were "and of right ought to be free

Salvation at Santiago

and independent." It also authorized the increase of the Regular Army to 62,597 men and the raising of a volunteer army of 125,000 men. As an act of diplomacy Negro troops would figure significantly in the liberation of the "colored" native Cuban.

Meanwhile, we had not solved our own racial problems. In spite of the impressive records made by colored military men in the past, race prejudice in the ranks prevailed in 1898 and often made life difficult for all-Negro units.

At Tampa, Florida, for example, colored troops were subjected to injustices aboard Havana-bound government transport ships. In port Teddy Roosevelt's white cavalrymen were given shore leave. The Negroes were not allowed off the ship except as marching units under white officers. They were assigned to the hold of the vessels in crowded, stuffy quarters. To make matters worse, they were wearing woolen uniforms designed for winter on the Great Plains. The colored men were not permitted to mingle on deck with white soldiers. Regardless of such discriminating treatment, once in action the Negroes fought gallantly.

On June 23, 1898, the black patriots engaged in their first battle on Cuban soil. At four-thirty a force of six thousand colored and white soldiers went ashore, regrouped, then marched to Las Guasimas, an outpost that the enemy had planned to abandon almost without a fight.

Stephen Bonal, a witness to the brief skirmish, said the moment an advance was ordered the colored troops of the Tenth forged ahead. They were no braver than any other men on the line, he said, but their better training prepared them for the engagement. The white cavalrymen were volunteers and lacked seasoned combat experience. Many were ex-cowboys, college athletes and adventurers. Colonel Roosevelt had had no previous military experience.

The Negroes, armed with semi-automatic weapons, were on the left and right of Teddy Roosevelt's Rough Riders in the advance on enemy fortifications. Defiantly they moved to the front of the American lines, pinning down the Spaniards with short, accurate shots from their guns.

Bonal said the combined force would have experienced a decisive victory over the Spaniards, but the Rough Riders did not have machine guns. "They were mislaid," he said. "At least the mules carrying them could not be found." Single shot rifles were no match for the faster-reacting semi-automatic weapons being used by the Negroes, and the diminishing Spanish defenses proved it.

In this fight Private Augustus Walley saved the life of a fellow cavalryman. He had already earned the

Salvation at Santiago

Medal of Honor for a similar feat eight years before. At that time, on August 16, 1881, the Marylander had rescued Private Burton from being killed by hostile Apaches in New Mexico. During the fight at Las Guasimas, Walley displayed the same daring and courage. He did not earn a medal for his latest humanitarian effort, but won the accolade of a grateful officer.

Walley was shooting his weapon from behind a bush when out of the corner of his eye he saw the image of one man seemingly struggling with another. The figures were Captain G. Ayers and Major B. F. Bell. The latter had been shot through the leg and the captain was trying to carry him to safety. In a death-defying run, dodging a hail of bullets trailing him for several yards, Private Walley went to the aid of his white superiors. From an enemy trench some distance away, Spanish riflemen hampered the rescue. Walley, standing tall, directed a burst of gunfire at the threatening stronghold. The Spanish guns fell silent. The Negro and the white captain carried Major Bell to safety.

Taking positions ahead of the American forces, the Tenth drove the Spaniards from their entrenchments. The fight was over. After the encounter there was a one-week lull in the fighting while the Americans prepared for the final assault up San Juan Hill to Santiago. Yet in spite of the tedious preparations, Colonel Roosevelt took time out to commend the Negroes for their gallantry at Las Guasimas. He said: "No troops could behave better than the colored soldiers." His remark was appropriate, but the utmost glory of the black patriots was yet to come.

At daybreak on June 30 the Americans opened a double attack on the enemy. The lesser drive was against a Spanish outpost at El Caney, well to the right. The major one was against enemy fortifications on San Juan Hill, as the series of high ridges before Santiago were called. The plan was to knock out El Caney's defenses in short time so that the troops dispatched against it would be able to participate in the action against Santiago.

Meanwhile at Tayabacoe, in the Cuban province of Puerto Principle, the transport ship *Florida* was maneuvering toward the horseshoe-shaped harbor. Aboard the vessel and her sister ship *Funita,* were fifty Negro cavalrymen of the Tenth and three hundred seventy-five Cubans. Their mission was to deliver ammunition and food for insurgents at Tunes near Cienfuegos. It was during this daring operation that four gallant, courageous colored men earned Medals of Honor.

After the ships had dropped anchor, a detachment of Cubans and several white Americans rowed to shore to survey enemy defenses. They secured their small boats and crept through the heavy brush. Without warning the Spaniards from a blockhouse several yards away fired on them. The men fought back, but were unable to penetrate the fortification. Overpowered, they decided to withdraw. Several of the Americans were wounded, five or six Cubans were killed in the retreat. When they reached a clearing, there before them were the remains of their boats. The Spaniards had destroyed them with well-directed artillery shells. Stranded, the detachment decided to hide under cover of approaching darkness near the surf and lagoon. They risked the possibility of being captured.

Aboard the *Florida*, Lieutenant C. P. Johnson heard the shots, but waited impatiently, hoping the landing party would return. After a short time and no sign of the men, he selected from the remaining Cubans a contingent of four rescue detachments. Each in turn rowed to the shore, but turned back. The missions proved too much of a challenge for them. Every attempted landing was thwarted by constant pounding by enemy gun positions in the blockhouse.

"My only hope is to try your colored boys," Johnson said to Lieutenant George P. Ahern. In the ship's hold, he told the weary Negroes about the men ashore, the repeated attempts to rescue them and the danger in carrying out a successful operation. An appeal was issued for volunteers.

Without hesitation, Privates Dennis Bell, Fitz Lee, William H. Thompkins and George H. Wanton agreed to attempt the rescue in spite of the risks. Bell was born in Washington, D. C.; Lee in Dinwiddie County, Virginia; and Thompkins and Wanton grew up together in Paterson, New Jersey.

The quartet, appreciating the fresh, salt air after being confined to the ship's hold, rowed cautiously to the shore, unchallenged. It was chilly. The group, like other cavalrymen, had thrown away their blankets because of the heat during the day. But at night the temperature dropped, and they wished for warmer garments, even while wearing winter uniforms.

As they dragged their boat ashore, the Spanish opened fire. Dropping to the wet sand, each in a prone position made his way through the darkness to the brush for cover. Projectiles resembling small meteors passed over their heads as they moved. Then the bombardment stopped as quickly as it had started. Now the only sounds were waves calmly rolling on the shore, insects and an occasional tropical bird calling its mate.

Quietly they moved through the brush not far from the shore line, searching for the missing men. A few yards away came a voice. "Hey, over here," someone called out in a whisper. Private Lee motioned for Thompkins to investigate. The others, weapons poised, stood by to cover him. His face glowing in the dark from perspiration, Thompkins moved cautiously toward the direction of the voice. "Who's thar?" he asked.

"Chandler," the voice replied, "over here."

Suspecting a trick, Thompkins hesitated, trying to de-
tect a flaw in the English the caller was speaking.
Quickly he remembered the lieutenant had mentioned
that a Winthrop Chandler was one of the missing men.
He still wasn't sure he would not be walking into a trap,
so he motioned for the others to move in closer. Wanton
stumbled over a body as he advanced, but said nothing.
Out of the darkness staggered two white men. "I'm
Chandler," one of them said. "Thank God, you found
us."

The greeting from the Spaniards was not as cordial.
From nearby bushes they peppered the American position with bullets. Assisting the wounded as best they
could, the detachment ran toward the shore. Two of the
Negroes remained temporarily to deter the attempted
assault. Then they too ran, joining the others and shooting at the enemy every few yards.

Safely reaching the boat, they rowed toward the
Florida. The enemy's bullets hit the water about them
like stones on the surface of a pond. Off in the distance
lay the *Florida*, her lights like distant stars, bobbing and
weaving as if suspended in the air. At about three
o'clock that morning, July 1, all were safely aboard the
transport ship.

Privates Bell, Lee, Thompkins and Wanton had risked
their lives and successfully performed a rescue mission

that had been thwarted on three previous occasions. They knew the dangers, yet they volunteered, demonstrating unflinching courage and devotion to duty. For their gallantry they were recommended for the Medal of Honor—the first of their race to be so honored during the war with Spain.

While the Tayabacoe heroes were resting from their ordeal on July 1, Teddy Roosevelt's Rough Riders were suffering defeat at El Caney. The garrison was well fortified, and the slopes below it were a tangle of bushes, vines and stunted trees reinforced with barbed wire. The approaches to the slopes were marshlands. Blockhouses guarded the hillside, and Spanish sharpshooters were concealed in the jungle undergrowth. The Rough Riders were unaware of the enemy's strength and strategic positions. They found themselves being attacked from all sides. Their casualties were heavy.

The colored Ninth and Tenth Cavalry units were not immediately ordered to take part in the fight. They were some distance away when notified of the disaster. The Negroes quickly regrouped and ran to aid their white comrades. Within minutes, they had joined the battle. Somewhere among them was Major Charles D. Young, the third Negro to graduate from West Point. He was leading the all-Negro Ninth Ohio Regiment.

The Negroes took positions in a wooded area. It seemed as though all the enemy's fire power was directed at the black patriots. Many were killed in the onslaught. In a short time they moved out of the woods, advancing relentlessly, all guns blazing. Despite the thick gray smoke, screaming shells and deadly bullets and a trail of dead and wounded, the Tenth forged ahead. Forward they marched, by the right flank, then to the left, until they arrived directly in front of the enemy, about one mile from its main defenses.

"Firing as they marched," a New York newspaper reported of the Tenth's advance, 'their aim was splendid, their coolness was superb, and their courage aroused the admiration of comrades."

The Negroes moved forward, in double time now, through the jungle and onward to the San Juan River. The artillery kept pace. "The atmosphere seemed perfectly alive with flying missiles from bursting shells overhead, and rifle bullets which seemed to have an explosive affect," Sergeant Baker said in his diary.

When the Negro troops neared the banks of the river their advance was slowed. A powerful barrage of Spanish shells and bullets bombarded the men. The artillery and infantry fire was coming from three blockhouses and a series of entrenchments in front and to the left of the invaders. The area was littered with dead and wounded men. Sometimes in confusion the troops became separated, but the front ranks were well preserved. The enemy fire was so intense that it sent the Negroes sprawling in the sand, digging for their lives with elbows and gun butts.

In the fracas Colonel T. A. Baldwin rode up and down the river bank rallying his men. Suddenly, a large shell exploded, knocking off the colonel's hat. His horse raised on its hind legs, throwing its rider onto the sandy beach. Sergeant Baker looked up just as the crippled animal fell. Through the smoke he saw Baldwin propped against a sand dune, holding his arm.

Sergeant Baker ran to the wounded officer, dodging bullets and exploding shells. Kneeling beside the colonel, Baker saw that shrapnel had entered the commander's arm and side. Baldwin insisted that the sergeant return to the lines. "I'm all right, Ed. Go back and rally the men," he said.

Baker hesitated, but he was obedient and, in a crouched position, moved to join the rest of his unit. There was no need to rally them. They were defiantly pounding the enemy with artillery and gunfire. Taking cover behind a clump of bushes near the river bank, Baker joined the fight.

Over the deafening sound of exploding shells and artillery booms, the sergeant heard a desperate cry for help. It was coming from the direction of the river. He looked through the thick smoke. There in the river a figure was struggling. The man was frantically trying to keep his head above water.

Immediately, Baker dropped his weapon and ran to

the soldier's aid. En route a shell barely missed hitting him. He dove for cover. Sand covered his perspiration-soaked face and shirt. "The shell passed so close I could feel the heat," he later recalled.

This close shave with death did not deter him. He jumped to his feet, sprinted for the river and through the waist-high water. The helpless soldier was Private Marshall. He had fallen in after being wounded by shell fragments. Baker, exposing himself to enemy fire, carried the wounded man to safety.

As the dispersed units began to link up, Baker joined his men and spent the rest of the day slogging it out beside them. The combined strength and aggressiveness of the colored cavalrymen and Roosevelt's men turned the tide of battle. They crushed the Spanish resistance at El Caney and steadily drove the remaining defenders toward Santiago.

Grateful Rough Riders were elated over the victory. One white corporal said: "If it had not been for the Negro cavalry, the Rough Riders would have been exterminated." A private remarked with all sincerity, "They can drink out of our canteens." And Teddy Roosevelt, just before the American Army took possession of Santiago on July 17, said: "I don't think that any Rough Rider will ever forget the tie that binds us to the Ninth and Tenth Cavalry."

Congress, in the name of the American people, showed its appreciation for the heroic deeds of Privates

Negro Medal of Honor Men

Bell, Lee, Thompkins, and Wanton by approving their superior's recommendations for Medals of Honor. On June 30, 1899, medals were awarded to the Tayabacoe heroes. At the time Bell and Thompkins were on occupation duty at Manzanillo, Cuba. Wanton was in his native Paterson, New Jersey, and Lee was hospitalized at Fort Bliss, Texas.

Sergeant Baker on August 2, 1898, was commissioned a second lieutenant in the Tenth U. S. Volunteer Infantry. Later he was confined to a hospital in Montana with an articular disease believed contracted in Cuba. For his noble self-sacrifice and courageous spirit at San Juan Hill he was, on July 3, 1902, awarded the Medal of Honor. At that time he was a lieutenant with the Philippine Indian Scouts, and stationed at Calamba Laguna near Manila. Baker retired after thirty years of military service while assigned to Fort McCowell, California, in January, 1910. He resided in Los Angeles and in 1913 died while a patient at Letterman General Hospital in San Francisco.

The year before the San Juan Hill hero was decorated, another Negro combatant who served in Cuba in 1898 earned a commission as second lieutenant. He was Benjamin O. Davis, Sr., a Regular Army cavalry officer, who in 1940 became the first of his race to attain the rank of brigadier general.

★

★

CHAPTER VII

Equality Achieved

Benjamin o. davis, sr. was promoted to first lieutenant in the Eighth U. S. Infantry after the Spanish-American War. But on March 6, 1899, he left military service and returned to civilian life. Later he regretted that decision and, on June 14, 1899, enlisted as a private with Troop I, Ninth Cavalry.

The following year he passed a competitive examination that made him eligible for a commission as second lieutenant. Just before President Theodore Roosevelt signed the commissioning order, an aide whispered that the candidate was a Negro. The President said: "Bully for him. Only one thing counts—he has qualified for the place."

Twelve years later, on December 18, 1912, the young lieutenant's son, Benjamin, Jr., was born in Washington,

D. C. He, too, eventually chose a military career and established himself as a distinguished officer.

In the meantime, the United States entered the war in Europe in April, 1917. The inevitable happened. Again there were national debates as to the utilization of 2,290,527 Negroes who had registered for the draft. Should a special camp be established solely for their training? Would any of them qualify for commissions as officers? If so, where would they be trained?

By midyear Camp Dodge, near Des Moines, Iowa, was designated the training site for Negro officers. On the fifteenth of October, 625 candidates had earned second lieutenant's commissions. In all, 458,839 Negro soldiers were initially trained and ready for service with the expeditionary forces.

The War Department established the Ninety-second and Ninety-third Divisions. These were almost totally made up of Negro officers and enlisted men. Of about 140,000 Negro troops sent to France, roughly 40,000 saw combat. The remainder of them carried brooms and shovels through the campaigns of World War I, even though they had been drilled for combat. Many American officers felt that Negroes were fit only for manual labor. Consequently a great number of colored doughboys spent their time in France as battalion laborers.

The fightingest colored infantry unit was by far the 369th Regiment. It was organized by Colonel William

Equality Achieved

Hayward as a challenge to prove Negroes could fight. On arriving at Camp Wadsworth, near Spartanburg, South Carolina, Hayward reportedly stood on the roof of one of the buildings and told his men this was their chance to show the people of Spartanburg and the world what educated Negroes were like. He begged them not to return violence, even if it were used against them by the townspeople.

In what was probably the first concept of the non-violent approach to racial unrest in the country, the Negroes heeded their colonel's plea. They took insults and beatings from the townspeople without retaliating. But Brigadier General Charles L. Phillips, who commanded Camp Wadsworth, decided the regiment should be moved in fairness to the men and to avoid a threatening explosion in the community. On January 1, 1918, the 369th landed in France and served directly under the French.

The regiment survived a collision at sea en route to Europe, but it became the first American unit to go into action. They were under fire for one hundred ninety-one days without relief, longer than any other United States regiment. Nevertheless they were the first of all Allied units to reach the Rhine. It was during this period that two Negroes of the 369th Infantry were the first American enlisted men, white or colored, to earn the French Croix de Guerre. The men were Sergeant

Negro Medal of Honor Men

Henry Johnson of New York City and Private Needham Roberts of Trenton, New Jersey.

Both soldiers were on duty as day was breaking on May 14, 1918. A group of Germans were discovered preparing to launch a sneak attack on an outpost at Butte de Mesnil. The enemy, finding that they had been discovered, threw a volley of grenades. Johnson, a former redcap at Grand Central Station in New York, was wounded three times. Roberts also was hit, but more seriously.

As the Germans rushed the Hell Fighters, as they called Negro doughboys, Johnson fired three cartridges from his bolt-action rifle. One of the foe fell with a bullet in his chest. Roberts, on the ground and bleeding from his wounds, painfully threw two grenades into the near darkness. About twenty Germans closed in and wrestled with the defenders. In the struggle, Roberts was overpowered and dragged off. By now Johnson had run out of ammunition. But he had to save his buddy. So with all the strength his slender frame could support, he used the rifle butt, knocking one of the Germans to the ground. Afterward he unveiled a bolo knife and hacked at the enemy while trying to rescue Roberts. When the fight ended, four Germans were dead and several others lay wounded. Johnson had rescued his badly wounded companion. He spent many weeks in the hospital as a result of wounds he received saving Roberts from becoming a prisoner of war.

Equality Achieved

Units of the Ninety-second Division were doing what they could to hasten victory in Europe, but they suffered handicaps that affected their fighting ability. The Ninety-second was under American command. It was poorly conditioned; its few Negro officers were far below the level of white officers in education and training. In addition French officers were asked not to permit "familiarity and indulgence" toward Negro officers; not to eat with them, shake hands with them or talk to them beyond military necessity. Situations like these had an adverse affect on the colored soldiers. The impact was so great that elements of the 366th Infantry Regiment reportedly became demoralized and fled to the rear during five days of the Meuse-Argonne offensive, which began on September 26, 1918.

The 366th, however, had its share of courageous men. Corporal Ed Merrifield was one of them. He earned the Distinguished Service Cross and Croix de Guerre for extraordinary heroism near Lesseau, France. In an attack similar to the one experienced by Sergeant Johnson and Private Roberts on May 14, Merrifield "although severely wounded, remained at his post and continued to fight a superior enemy force, beating off a raid."

While the Meuse-Argonne offensive was in progress, two men of the 372nd Infantry earned the Croix de Guerre with Palm, the Distinguished Service Cross, and the Medaille Militaire. It happened on September 27 and 28, 1918. Of the engagement, War Department records show:

> Corporal Clifton Merimon of Cambridge, Massachusetts, was near Bussey Farm, France. He made an attack with hand grenades on an enemy machine gun which was killing and wounding the men of his platoon. The wiry corporal succeeded in killing the gunner and putting the weapon out of commission. Later he reorganized the remainder of his unit and led them south of the farm. In spite of being gassed, he single-handedly knocked out another machine gun emplacement.

The following day gruelling fire from hidden automatic weapons nests continued to harass the 372nd Infantry. But Corporal Clarence R. Van Alen of Boston, Massachusetts, was determined to prevent the continued slaughter of his comrades. Finding one enemy position, he charged it, killing four of the gunners and taking three others as prisoners. He suffered only a few scratches in the skirmish; at least they were not serious enough to put him out of action. Later Van Alen, again single-handedly, captured a trench mortar battery that was inflicting severe losses on the French.

Such were some of the heroic deeds performed by Negro doughboys during World War I. Some of the proudest records of American bravery were compiled *en masse* and individually by black patriots during World War I. The 369th Infantry was cited eleven times for bravery and was awarded the Croix de Guerre as a unit in addition to 171 individual citations. The 370th fought the last battle of the war, capturing a German wagon train a half hour after the Armistice had been signed. Its sister regiment, the 371st, was the only infantry unit to shoot down three German planes. Combined, the 370th and 371st earned 191 Croix de Guerre and 43 Distinguished Service Crosses. No Negroes received the Medal of Honor during World War I.

In spite of these impressive accomplishments many false charges of incompetence and inefficiency were leveled against Negro regiments. Records show that many of the charges were against colored officers by white commanders who did not desire to serve with them. Major General Robert Lee Bullard, World War I commander of the Second Army, which included the Ninety-second Division, said in his memoirs, according to author Lee Nichols, that Negroes were emotionally unsuited for war. He said they were "lazy, slothful, superstitious, imaginative. . . . if you need combat soldiers, and especially if you need them in a hurry, don't put your time upon Negroes."

Secretary of War Newton D. Baker came to the Negroes' defense by saying the circumstances of the reported retreat in the Meuse-Argonne offensive "do not justify many of the highly colored accounts which have been given of the behavior of the troops in this action, and they afford no basis at all for any of the general assumptions with regard to the action of colored troops in this battle and elsewhere in France."

There were many charges and countercharges, but the Negro units were quickly moved from France and deactivated after the Armistice was signed. Only a handful of high-ranking colored officers remained in uniform, among them Lieutenant Colonel Benjamin O. Davis, Sr. There were no Negro officers commissioned in the U. S. Navy during World War I.

No significant Negro advances in the military occurred until 1936. On June 12 of that year Colonel Davis' son Benjamin, Jr. walked up to General John J. Pershing at West Point, saluted and received his diploma and a commission as a second lieutenant in the U. S. Army. Young Davis became the first Negro since Charles D. Young, forty-seven years before, to graduate from the U. S. Military Academy. He had entered West Point in 1932 after being recommended for attendance by Congressman Oscar DePriest of Chicago. Most of Davis' four years at the school were spent in segregation. He lived alone, while white students shared two-man rooms. Upperclassmen tried to force him out by giving him the silent treatment. They gave him demerits for such things as imaginary flecks of dust on his shoes. Yet he stood thirty-fifth in his graduating class of two hundred seventy-six officers. His first assignment in

Equality Achieved

1936 was as Commander, F Company, Twenty-fourth Infantry at Fort Benning, Georgia.

Young Davis was a captain and professor of military science at Tuskegee Institute, Alabama, when his father was promoted to brigadier general. This was in 1940, the year President Franklin D. Roosevelt signed the Selective Service Act, which contained a clause barring racial discrimination toward men drafted into the armed forces.

In 1941 Captain Davis broke the Army Air Corps color barrier. Negroes, up to that time, were not accepted for pilot training because military men believed that colored men "lacked technical ability to fly planes." In May of that year young Davis became one of the first of his race to take advance flying training. Later he was to assume command of the Ninety-ninth Pursuit Squadron, the first Negro air unit in United States history.

Meanwhile, a colored seaman became the first hero of World War II. He was Doris Miller, a Messman First Class serving aboard the U. S. S. *Arizona* when the Japanese attacked the United States. The battleship was anchored in Pearl Harbor on Sunday, December 7, 1941. Miller, born at Waco, Texas, October 12, 1919, was on the deck when a formation of airplanes approached. One of them peeled off and dove toward the *Arizona.* As it passed over the battleship, the pilot released a bomb, then pulled back on the control stick and headed for the blue sky.

The explosion knocked Miller down. As he scrambled to his feet the rumble of other blasts and the chatter of machine guns broke the serenity of the otherwise lazy day. Looking around as smoke and flames dominated the once scenic Pearl Harbor, he spotted someone lying on the captain's bridge.

He ran to the spot. The wounded man was his commander. There was blood on the deck from chest and stomach injuries. Miller had no way of stopping the steady flow of blood, so he decided to move the captain to a safer place and look for the medic. Lifting the man carefully, he started across the bridge and down a ladder. As he moved toward a companionway, bullets from an enemy plane ripped splinters of wood from the deck about him.

Behind the companionway, he placed the officer on the deck near the steel bulkhead. While other sailors and a medical corpsman treated the captain, Miller made his way across the bridge to a machine gun.

Miller was a messman. As such he was not permitted to fire a gun. As a matter of fact, he had never been instructed in the use of a weapon. But this was no time to be concerned about navy regulations. Bullets spattered around him, bombs were falling, and explosions were ripping ship after ship. Miller revolved the machine

Equality Achieved

gun on its base and squeezed the trigger as another plane made a pass. Nothing happened. Reacting like a seasoned artilleryman, he pulled back twice on the weapon's charging handle to release the jam, then fired continuous bursts at an attacking aircraft. His first target burst into flames and plummeted into the harbor.

In the ensuing assault Miller shot down at least three more planes until his ammunition was exhausted. By now the *Arizona* was sinking, and the courageous son of a sharecropper was ordered from the bridge.

"For his distinguished devotion to duty, extraordinary courage and disregard of his own personal safety . . ." Doris Miller earned the Navy Cross. On June 10, 1942, Admiral Chester W. Nimitz pinned the Navy's highest award for valor on the twenty-one-year-old Negro's chest. The following year, on November 24, the carrier *Liscome Bay* sank at sea after a torpedo struck her amidships. She went to the bottom of the Pacific Ocean with most of her 712-man crew. Among them was Doris Miller.

Meanwhile the War Department had reactivated the Ninety-second Division as an all-Negro infantry unit. But unlike its predecessor organization its combatants were better educated, better trained and had better leadership. In Europe during World War II the division was responsible for many victories. As a result the Negro officer gained full recognition as a hero.

Negro Medal of Honor Men

There were 469 Medals of Honor awarded for unyielding courage during World War II, but none went to Negroes. The highest award for gallantry earned by colored officers and enlisted men during that conflict was the Distinguished Service Cross. A War Department press release of October, 1945, lists 273 awards made to colored men. These include the Silver Star, the Distinguished Flying Cross, the Soldier's Medal, the Bronze Star Medal and the Air Medal.

Lieutenant (later captain) Charles Thomas of Detroit, Michigan, earned the Distinguished Service Cross for gallantry near Climbach, France. He was at the time a tank commander with the 614th Tank Destroyer Battalion.

The Ninety-second Division had its share of heroes. Over three thousand men from that unit were killed, wounded and missing in the Rome campaign. War Department records show that sixty-five men received Silver Stars and as many were given Bronze Star Medals. Another thirteen hundred earned Purple Heart Medals. The Distinguished Service Cross was awarded to First Lieutenant Vernon Baker for destroying enemy installations, personnel and equipment near Viareggio, Italy. Second Lieutenant (later lieutenant colonel) Reuben Horner earned the Silver Star; so did Captain Charles F. Gandy, and Lieutenants John Madison and Kenneth W. Coleman, posthumously.

Equality Achieved

Gandy had earlier received an on-the-spot promotion to captain from General Mark W. Clark following a review of division troops near Leghorn, Italy. The former Fifth Army Commander later became a chief advocate of integration in the armed forces.

The 366th Infantry Regiment, as if trying to rectify its World War I namesake's retreat during the Meuse-Argonne offensive, fought gallantly in Italy during the Second World War. Its Silver Star winners, according to a War Department press announcement, included First Lieutenant William E. Porter, a platoon leader in Company B; Captain James L. Jones of Dallas, Texas, while serving as a chaplain with a quartermaster unit on the Anzio beachhead; and Captain Royall B. Fleming, a medical officer near Viareggio.

While Negroes were making impressive combat records in Europe, the Ninety-ninth Pursuit Squadron at Tuskegee Army Air Base, Alabama, was changing the views of those who said "Negroes lacked the technical ability to fly planes." Their training "experiment" was becoming a reality. By April, 1943, the unit was in French Morocco for training under experienced combat pilots. The following month Captain Davis was promoted to major, then lieutenant colonel—all in one day.

Later the squadron moved to Sicily. Its first mission was over an enemy base at Fardjouna. In the Department of Defense pamphlet, *Integration and the Negro*

111

Negro Medal of Honor Men

Officer in the Armed Forces, it is reported that Lieutenant Charles B. Hall of Brazil, Indiana, on July 2, 1943, shot down the first German plane officially credited to the squadron. Two of the Ninety-ninth's aircraft were lost that day, but the lieutenant destroyed the Focke-Wulf 190 and was awarded the Distinguished Flying Cross. The medal was the Air Corps' highest decoration.

In October, 1943, Davis was recalled to the United States and placed in command of the all-Negro 332nd Fighter Group at Lockbourne Army Air Base, near Columbus, Ohio. For three months he used his combat experience to mold the unit, which boasted the highest percentage of college graduates in the armed forces, into one of the best fighter outfits in the Air Corps. It moved to Italy in December, 1943, and five months later Davis was promoted to full colonel.

The 332nd went to Europe to protect United States bombers from being attacked and shot down by enemy fighters. Yet it was not until January, 1944, that the Negro airmen really achieved prominence. At that time the 332nd shot down sixteen German Messerschmitts and Focke-Wulfs over the bitterly contested Anzio beachhead. *Time* magazine, on February 14, 1944, said: "Any outfit would have been proud of the record. These victories stamped the final seal of combat excellence on one of the most controversial outfits in the Army, the all-Negro fighter squadron."

Equality Achieved

During the Italian campaign Colonel Davis and his men overcame such obstacles as tricky air currents over mountain ranges and operating from far-flung bases on limited fuel and ammunition. In spite of these odds, and notwithstanding enemy fighter attacks, the 332nd chalked up impressive victories. In its two hundred escort missions it never lost a bomber to German aircraft fire.

One of its most successful encounters occurred on March 24, 1945. While escorting a B-17 bomber force on a raid on Berlin, the 332nd downed three German planes, probably destroyed another three and damaged three more without losing a single plane of its own. Eight highly rated enemy jets were reported to have been knocked down that day. For this "extraordinary heroism in action" the unit was awarded the Distinguished Unit Citation.

By the end of the war Colonel Davis and his men had earned numerous awards for their daring and fortitude. Unconfirmed reports show that more than one hundred Distinguished Flying Crosses were recommended for Negro pilots during World War II.

The 332nd Fighter Group left Europe in June, 1945. Colonel Davis had earned the Air Medal with four Oak Leaf Clusters, the Distinguished Flying Cross, the Legion of Merit with one Oak Leaf Cluster and the Silver Star. The latter was awarded for "gallantry in action" while leading a squadron of P-51 fighters on a hazard-ous mission against air fields in southern Germany.

Following World War II, an Army board under the direction of Lieutenant General Alvan C. Gillem, Jr. studied Negro participation in the war and submitted a report on *The Utilization of Negro Manpower in the Postwar Army.* This document led to the 1946 policy announcement assuring Negroes a continuing place in the military. It recommended elimination of the all-Negro Ninety-second Division and the grouping of Negro and white units of similar size into composite organizations.

Two years later, President Truman issued Executive Order 9981, dated July 26, 1948, establishing the Fahy Committee. He charged the group with the responsibil-ity of examining all existing regulations and practices regarding military personnel. The President wanted to put into effect a national policy of "equality of treat-ment and opportunity for all persons in the Armed Services without regard to race, color, religion or na-tional origin." The report of this committee, entitled *Freedom to Serve,* was submitted to President Truman in 1950. It provided the philosophy and working basis for racial integration with no restrictions as to racial quotas.

In the meantime, while the Fahy Committee was at work, Brigadier General Benjamin O. Davis, Sr. retired from active duty. His decorations and awards at that time, in addition to those received in action, included the Bronze Star, the French Croix de Guerre and the Distinguished Service Medal.

The Air Force (which until the National Security Act of 1947 was known as the Army Air Corps) began putting into effect an integration policy approved by Secretary of Defense Louis Johnson. As the first step, a board of officers, on which Colonel Benjamin O. Davis, Jr. served, in May, 1949, began screening the records of three thousand Negro officers and airmen at Lockbourne Air Force Base. Those men considered suitable for immediate assignment to existing units were shipped to air bases throughout the world. Others with potential aptitude were sent to schools to learn technical skills. A few did not measure up to standard, so they were honorably discharged.

Defense Secretary Johnson's desegregation order, according to Colonel Davis, was received with mixed reactions. Some of the men were reluctant to being uprooted and assigned to different environments. Many did not know how they would be treated as members of previously all-white units. However, "the largest percentage of the men considered the change a challenge and were eager to correct a long injustice," the colonel said.

"We integrated by moving all the men out of the barracks and reassigned them to quarters by alphabet regardless of race," said Lieutenant Colonel George J. Friedline, a white officer who commanded a segregated unit at Andrews Field, Maryland.

In June, 1949, a month after the Lockbourne Air Force Base desegregation board met, Ensign Wesley A. Brown became the first Negro to graduate from the U. S. Naval Academy. Later that year a high-ranking U. S. Army officer was quoted as saying that in the Air Force airmen are airmen, but the Negro in the Army is a Negro.

This was generally the attitude of the Army's top brass. Some feared integration because of pressures from the southerner, others objected to change—any change. There was, however, some progress toward desegregation, and by mid-1950 the breakthrough came. The urgent need for men to halt aggression in Korea gradually eliminated segregation, and the Negro made advances in military society.

When Dwight D. Eisenhower became President, on January 20, 1952, he reaffirmed President Truman's policy of "equality of treatment and opportunity" in the military establishment. On March 19, 1952, he told a news conference he did not approve of any discrimination in the use of federal funds. Six days later he announced steps toward ending segregation in schools for servicemen's children on military posts. The following

Equality Achieved

year, on May 9, 1953, President Eisenhower told a United Negro College Fund luncheon he "passionately" believed in equality regardless of race or color and that to the extent that there was recognition of "second class citizens," all others became less than first class.

Colonel Davis, in November, 1953, assumed command of the Fifty-first Fighter-Interceptor Wing at Suwon, Korea. A year later he was promoted to brigadier general. He was, as his father had been, the ranking Negro in the military. General Davis was commanding Air Task Force Thirteen (Provisional), a surface-to-air missile unit, on Formosa when the Chinese Communists began shelling Nationalist China's islands of Quemoy and Matsu. That was in 1955, the year the Office of the Civilian Assistant to the Secretary of Defense reported:

> . . . The accelerated impetus of the program of racial integration in the Armed Forces during the postwar years has given Negro personnel the opportunity to demonstrate their skill and ability without limitations imposed by race. Better utilization has improved Service effectiveness. . . . many Negroes in uniform are now holding responsible and important positions on a fully integrated basis . . .

While Deputy Chief of Staff for Operations, United States Air Forces, Europe, in 1959, General Davis was promoted to major general. Six years later, on April 30, 1965, he was advanced to lieutenant general. A few days

117

afterward he was sent to Korea as Chief of Staff, United Nations Command, to coordinate all activities of the UN peace-keeping mission there.

In the meantime, the Negro was making unheralded progress in the military. Unlike the black patriots of the Civil War, Indian campaigns and the Spanish-American War, this new breed of fighting man was better educated and prepared to take on technological duties in the defense establishment.

Lieutenant Commander Samuel L. Gravely, on January 31, 1962, was given command of the destroyer U. S. S. *Falgout.* This marked the first time a Negro officer had been given command of a ship in the modern Navy. In June of the same year Captain Edward J. Dwight, a native of Kansas City, Kansas, was selected from more than one hundred applicants for entry into the Aerospace Research Pilot School. This was a stepping-stone toward entering the U. S. Manned Space Flight Program. He did not complete astronaut training, but later served as an experimental flight test officer for the Air Force Systems Command.

By October, 1962, the Cold War became hot. Negroes again played significant roles in the defense of freedom.

During the Cuban crisis, Captain Thomas L. Hennagan flew jet reconnaissance missions over Cuba when the Soviet Union established offensive missile sites there. "For exemplary courage and professional competence

Equality Achieved

. . . under hazardous flight conditions," Hennagan was awarded the Distinguished Flying Cross, then the Air Force's highest decoration.

While Captain Hennagan was photographing Cuban territory from thousands of feet in the air at supersonic speed, Negro combat crewmen stood alert in Minuteman missile sites sixty feet below the surface on the ground on the mainland. In the event of hostilities, on the word of the President, these men could send tons of TNT soaring toward predesignated enemy targets.

When world tension shifted from the Caribbean to Southeast Asia, the Negro was among the earliest on the scene. Captain Joseph S. Grant, Jr. became one of the first of his race to assist the South Vietnamese in their fight for freedom in the face of Communist aggression. He was a member of an advisory team sent to Vietnam to train South Vietnamese Air Force pilots in combat-support operations against the northern invaders.

In the United States there remained citizens who were concerned with the treatment of Negro military men. President John F. Kennedy ordered a study on equality of treatment and opportunity for Negro military personnel. After the Honorable Gerhard A. Gasell, chairman of the President's Committee on Equal Opportunity in the Armed Forces, submitted his findings in June, 1963, the President said:

Negro Medal of Honor Men

> . . . the Armed Forces has made significant progress in eliminating discrimination among those serving in the defense of the Nation. . . . Much remains to be done . . . in eliminating practices that cause inconvenience and embarrassment to servicemen and their families in communities adjoining military bases.

But the mere performance of an assigned responsibility can, at least temporarily, lower racial barriers in some communities. This was the case with Air Force Captain Keaver Holley III.

In Brownfield, Texas, Holley, braving intense heat and high winds for over half an hour, piloted a helicopter that rescued an injured worker from a three-hundred-foot grain elevator shaft.

To show their appreciation for his daring, the city held a dinner in the Negro's honor. Holley and his wife set a precedent at the affair by being seated at the head table with civic leaders in a community that practiced strict segregation.

In September, 1965, another Negro helicopter pilot performed an act of valor and heroism involving voluntary risk of life. He was Captain John A. Darden of El Dorado, Arkansas. Darden and a white companion, Captain Robert S. Henderson of Flint, Michigan, saved twelve lives and rescued twenty-five during floods in Italy.

The captains, assigned to an Aerospace Recovery and

Equality Achieved

Rescue Detachment at Avion Air Base, flew missions continuously in a two-day period under extremely hazardous conditions.

Three times Captains Henderson and Darden hovered with rotor blades only inches from television antennae to recover six persons from their homes. Later, Darden, the copilot, saved the life of an aging man who had been swept into a flooded stream. The Negro was lowered from the helicopter and, while suspended, carried the man over the rampaging waters to safety.

The two pilots earned the Cheney Award, presented annually for an act of valor, extreme fortitude or self-sacrifice in a humanitarian interest, performed in connection with aircraft. They received a bronze plaque and certificate and shared a five-hundred-dollar award.

In April, 1966, the Navy announced promotion of its first Negro to captain (that service's equivalent of full colonel). He was Thomas D. Parham, Jr. of Newport News, Virginia. Parham was a chaplain assigned to Quonset Point, Rhode Island, Naval Air Station at the time. The Marine Corps, a component of the Navy Department, however, had no Negroes serving above company grade at this time.

A month before the Navy announced the precedent-setting promotion of Chaplain Parham, the Department of Defense revealed that of the United States military personnel in the Vietnamese War, proportionately more

Negro Medal of Honor Men

Negroes than whites had died. The figures, compiled in a Pentagon survey, showed that at the end of 1965, 1,424 Army and Marine Corps officers and enlisted men had been killed. Of that number 236 were Negroes. The Navy was unable to come up with precise figures, but estimated its number of Negroes in and off Vietnam at 500, with only one Negro death in four years. The Air Force reported 908 Negroes and no Vietnam deaths.

The Defense Department released these figures after Congressmen had raised questions about whether Negroes were discriminated against on the battlefield. And some civil rights leaders had protested that Negroes were forced to fight a war with which they were not in sympathy.

Two of the congressmen concerned over the accusations were from the South. This in itself was significant. For in past wars and conflicts few whites, much less southerners, voiced concern nationally about the welfare of Negro combatants.

During the Senate hearing in March, 1966, Senator Richard Russell of Georgia said some constituents had complained that Negroes were being assigned "in disproportionate numbers to the most dangerous areas in Vietnam."

General Earle G. Wheeler, chairman of the Joint Chiefs of Staff, had just returned from Vietnam and denied this, saying: "I noted about the same proportion

Equality Achieved

of colored troops in the forward areas that you would expect. I didn't notice either any unusually large numbers of Negroes or lesser number of whites."

Senator Allen J. Ellender of Louisiana asked General Wheeler about "the proportion of Negroes to whites in a combat unit."

"You will find that in certain airborne units the [number of] Negro soldiers will run as high as 18 per cent. In most units you will probably find it is around 13 or 14 percent," the general replied.

Brigadier General Ellis W. Williamson, who commanded the 173rd Brigade in Vietnam, said his unit had no more Negroes than other units in Vietnam.

Defense and congressional officials finally dismissed the accusations, because the figures released were only estimates. As integration advanced in the military service, race was eliminated from many personnel records. Orders reassigning troops from one duty station to another contain a man's name, rank, serial number, destination and other pertinent data. Whether he is white or colored is not recorded.

Perhaps the best explanation for the Vietnamese discrimination charges was the fact that Negroes were among the highest numbers to volunteer for longer military careers. But, as one Pentagon spokesman said, if the figures show anything "it is the valor of the Negro in combat."

Negro Medal of Honor Men

To accentuate that valor, President Lyndon B. Johnson, at 12:15 P.M. on April 21, 1966, awarded the Medal of Honor posthumously to Private First Class Milton L. Olive III.

The medal was presented to the soldier's father, Milton B. Olive, Jr. of Chicago. This was the third Medal of Honor awarded in the Vietnam War and the first to a Negro who fought in Vietnam.

Private Olive was a member of the Third Platoon of Company B. Second Battalion (Airborne), 503rd Infantry, as it moved through the jungle to find the Viet Cong operating in the vicinity of Phu Cuong on October 22, 1965. Although the platoon was subjected to a heavy volume of enemy gunfire and pinned down temporarily, it retaliated by assaulting the Viet Cong positions, causing the enemy to flee.

As the platoon pursued the insurgents, Private Olive and four other soldiers were moving through the jungle together when a grenade was thrown into their midst. Private Olive saw the grenade and then saved the lives of his fellow soldiers at the sacrifice of his own by grabbing the grenade in his hand and falling on it to absorb the blast with his body.

Immediately on being notified of his twenty-year-old son's extraordinary heroism and award of the Medal of Honor, Mr. Olive wrote President Johnson. In his letter he said:

Equality Achieved

Our only child and only grandchild gave his last full measure of devotion on an international battlefield 10,000 miles from home. It is our dream and prayer that some day the Asiatics, the Europeans, the Israelites, the Africans, the Australians, the Latins, and the Americans can all live in One-World. It is our hope that in our own country the Klansmen, the Negroes, the Hebrews, and the Catholics will sit down together in the common purpose of good will and dedication; that the moral and creative intelligence of our united people will pick up the chalice of wisdom and place it upon the mountain top of human integrity; that all mankind, from all the earth, shall resolve, "to study war no more." That, Mr. President, is how I feel and that is my eternal hope for our Great American Society.

Appendix

CIVIL WAR

First Sergeant Powhatan Beaty—April 6, 1865
Private William H. Barnes—April 6, 1865
First Sergeant James H. Bronson—April 6, 1865
Sergeant William H. Carney—May 23, 1900
Sergeant Decatur Dorsey—November 8, 1865
Sergeant Major Christian A. Fleetwood—April 6, 1865
Private James Gardiner—April 6, 1865
Sergeant James H. Harris—February 18, 1874
Sergeant Major Thomas Hawkins—February 8, 1870
Sergeant Alfred B. Hilton—April 6, 1865

Appendix

Sergeant Major Milton M. Holland—April 6, 1865
Corporal Miles James—April 6, 1865
First Sergeant Alexander Kelly—April 6, 1865
First Sergeant Robert Pinn—April 6, 1865
First Sergeant Edward Ratcliff—April 6, 1865
Private Charles Veal—April 6, 1865

INDIAN CAMPAIGNS

Sergeant Thomas Boyne—January 6, 1882
Sergeant Benjamin Brown—February 19, 1890
Sergeant John Denny—November 27, 1894
Corporal Clinton Greaves—June 26, 1879
Sergeant Henry Johnson—September 22, 1890
Sergeant George Jordan—May 7, 1890
Corporal Isaiah Mays—February 19, 1890
Sergeant William McBryar—May 15, 1890
Sergeant Emanuel Stance—June 28, 1870
Private Augustus Walley—October 1, 1890
First Sergeant Moses Williams—November 12, 1896
Corporal William O. Wilson—September 17, 1891
Sergeant Brent Woods—July 12, 1894

SPANISH-AMERICAN WAR

Sergeant Major Edward L. Baker—July 3, 1902
Sergeant Dennis Bell—June 23, 1899
Private Fitz Lee—June 23, 1899
Sergeant William H. Thompkins—June 23, 1899
Private George H. Wanton—June 23, 1899

Appendix

KOREAN CONFLICT

Sergeant Cornelius H. Charlton—March 12, 1952
Private First Class William Thompson—June 21, 1951

VIETNAM WAR

Private First Class Milton L. Olive III—April 26, 1966

NAVY MEDALS OF HONOR

Landsman Aaron Anderson—June 22, 1865
Ship's Cook Daniel Atkins—May 20, 1898
Landsman Robert Blake—April 16, 1864
Landsman John Lawson—December 31, 1864
Seaman Joseph B. Noil—1873
Seaman Joachim Pease—December 31, 1864
Fireman Robert Penn—December 14, 1898

Bibliography

Air Force Manual 35–10. *Service and Dress Uniforms for Air Force Personnel,* Washington, D.C.: Government Printing Office, 1963.

Beyer, Walter F. and O. F. Keydel, eds. *Deeds of Valor.* Detroit: Perrien-Keydel Co., 1903.

Bureau of Personnel. *Medal of Honor, the Navy* (1861–1949). Washington, D.C.: Government Printing Office, 1950.

Decorations and Awards of the Army. Department of the Army. Washington, D.C.: Government Printing Office, 1947.

Integration and the Negro Officer in the Armed Forces of the United States. Department of Defense. Washington, D.C.: Government Printing Office, 1962.

Glass, Edward L. N. *History of the Tenth Cavalry, 1866–1921.* Arizona, 1921.

Initial Report: *Equality of Treatment and Opportunity for Negro Military Personnel Stationed Within the United States.* Washington, D.C.: 1963.

Medal of Honor of the U. S. Army. Washington, D.C.: Government Printing Office, 1948.

131

Bibliography

Medal of Honor of the Navy (1861–1948). Washington, D.C.: Government Printing Office, 1949.

Navy and Marine Corps Awards Manual. Department of the Navy. Washington, D.C.: Government Printing Office, 1953.

Subcommittee on Veterans' Affairs of the Committee on Labor and Public Welfare. United States Senate. Washington, D.C.: Government Printing Office, 1964.

Annual Reports of the Secretary of War (1846–1891). War Department. Washington, D.C.: Government Printing Office, 1892.

War of the Rebellion. A Compilation of the Official Records of the Union and Confederate Armies. Washington, D.C.: 1880–1891.

Williams, George W. *A History of the Negro Troops in the War of the Rebellion, 1861–1865.* New York: Harper and Brothers, 1888.

Index

Aerospace Research Pilot School, 118

Ahern, Lt. George P., 91

Air Force, integration policy initiated by, 115-116

Air Force Systems Comand, 118

Air Task Force Thirteen (Provisional), 117

Alabama, 42-45

Allen, Regimental Adjutant George, 30

Anderson, Landsman Aaron, 48-50

Andrews, John, 20

Andrews Field, Md., 116

Annapolis
first Negro entrant, 50
first Negro graduate, 116

Anzio beachead, 111, 112

Apache campaign, 63-66, 70, 71-76

Apaches, 84

Army, integration of, 116

Army Air Corps, breaking of color barrier, 107

Atkins, Ship's Cook First Class Daniel, 50-53

Ayers, Capt. G., 89

Baker, Sgt. Maj. Edward L., 76, 84, 85, 95-98

Baker, Henry B., 50

Baker, Secretary of War Newton D., 105

Baker, First Lt. Vernon, 110

Baldwin, Col. T. A., 96

Banks, Gen. Nathaniel P., 19

Barnes, Pvt. William H., 29

Beaty, First Sgt. Powhatan, 33

Bell, Maj. B. F., 89

Bell, Pvt. Dennis, 91-94, 98

Benefield, Second Lt. William H., 13

Beyers, Capt. Charles D., 64

Big Foot, 81, 82

Birney, Maj. Gen. D. B., 27, 29

Blake, Robert, 35-38, 41-42

Boernstein, Maj. A. S., 30

Bonal, Stephen, 88

Boyne, Sgt. Thomas, 63, 64, 66

Bradley, Omar N., 9, 10

Breckenridge, Ensign Joseph C., 51-53

"Brevet" system of promotion, 3

133

Index

Bronson, First Sgt. James H., 33
Bronze Service Star, 15
Brown, Sgt. Benjamin, 12, 78-80
Brown, Ensign Jesse L., 14
Brown, Ensign Wesley A., 116
Brown, Landsman Wilson, 46-47
Brownfield, Tex., Negro helicopter pilot honored in, 120
Buffalo Bill (William F. Cody), 5
Bullard, Maj. Gen. Robert Lee, 105
Bureau of Colored Troops (1863), 22
Burnett, Second Lt. George R., 71-73, 75
Burnside, Maj. Gen. Ambrose, 28
Burton, Pvt. 73, 74, 89
Butler, Gen. Benjamin F., 20, 29-30
Butler medals, design of, 34
Byrd, Commodore Richard E., Jr., 2

Camp Dodge, Iowa, 100
Camp Wadsworth, S. C., 101
Camp William Penn, 21
Cappage, Frank, 51
Carney, Sgt. William H., 21, 24-26
Carroll, Capt. Henry, 60
Catch-the-Bear, 81
Certificate of Merit, 2-3
discontinued, 5
Chaffin's Farm, battle of, 28, 30, 32-34
Chandler, Winthrop, 92
Charlton, Sgt. Cornelius H., 10, 15-17
Charlton family, 17
Cheney Award, 121
Chiricahua Indians, 61-62
Chuchillo Negro Mountains, battle of, 71-75
Civil War, 2, 4, 19-34

Negro casualties during, 40
nondiscrimination in Navy during, 39
unequal pay for Negroes during, 23
Clark, Gen. Mark W., 111
Climbach, France, 110
Cody, William F. (Buffalo Bill), 5
Coleman, Lt. Kenneth W., 110
Combat Infantryman Badge, 11
Congressional Medal of Honor (see Medal of Honor)
Conyers, James H., 50
Croix de Guerre, 103, 105
awarded to first Americans, 101-102
Croix de Guerre with Palm, 103
Cuba, Santiago campaign in, 84-98
Cuban crisis (1962), 118-119
Curtin, Andrew, 21

Daly, George, 76
Darden, Capt. John A., 120-121
Davis, Brig. Gen. Benjamin O., Jr., 99-100, 111-115, 117-118
awards to, 113-114
as Chief of Staff, U. N. Command, in Korea, 118
treatment at West Point, 106-107
Davis, Brig. Gen. Benjamin O., Sr., 98, 99, 106, 114-115, 117
awards to, 115
Day, Lt. Matthias W., 66
Decorations, order of precedence, 8
Deep Bottom, Va., battle of, 27
Denny, Sgt. John, 63, 65-66
DePriest, Oscar, 106
Design
of Medal of Honor, 6-7

Index

Distinguished Flying Cross, 112, 119
Distinguished Service Cross, 5-6, 13, 17, 103, 105, 110
Distinguished Service Medals, 6
Distinguished Unit Citation, to 332nd Fighter Group, 113
Dix, Maj. Gen. John Adam, 23-24, 39, 40
Dodge, Capt. Francis S., 68
Dorsey, Sgt. Decatur, 27-28
Douglass, Frederick, 21
Dudley, Lt. Col. N. A. M., 64-65
Dwight, Capt. Edward L., 118

Eisenhower, Dwight D., 116, 117
El Chaney, battle of, 90, 94-97
Ellender, Allen J., 123
Emancipation Proclamation, 20
Equality for Negro in 20th century, 99-124
Everetts, John, 51-53

Fahy Committee, 114
Farragut, Rear Adm. David G., 45
Fifth U. S. Colored Troops, 30, 32
    organization of, 33
Fifty-first Fighter-Interceptor Wing, 117
Fifty-fourth U. S. Colored Infantry, 31
First Volunteer Cavalry (Rough Riders), 85, 88, 94, 97
503rd Infantry, 124
Fleetwood, Sgt. Maj. Christian A., 23, 27, 30-32
Fleming, Capt. Royall B., 111
Flipper, Henry O., 61
Florida, 90, 91, 93
Florida Mountains of New Mexico, 61
Formosa, 117

Fort Bliss, Tex., 98
Fort Cummings, N. M., 59
Fort Fisher, N. C., 4, 23
Fort Gaines, 46
Fort Grant, 78
Fort Harrison, battle of, 28
Fort Jackson, 4
Fort Leavenworth, Kans., 86
Fort McKavett, 60
Fort Morgan, 46
Fort Powell, 46
Fort Robinson, Neb., 57, 59, 66
Fort Russell, 69
Fort St. Philip, 4
Fort Steele, 67
Fort Thomas, 78
Fort Tulerso, N. M., 70
Fort Wagner, S. C., 24
Fourth U. S. Colored Troops, 30, 31
Freedom to Serve, 114
Freeland, Pvt., 64
French Morocco, 111
Friedline, Lt. Col. George J., 116
Funita, 90

Gaballan Canyon, battle of, 76-77, 84
Gandy, Capt. Charles F., 110-111
Gardiner, Pvt. James, 29
Gasell, Gerhard A., 119
Georgia, Mitchell's raid through, 4
Gibbon, W. T., 78, 79
Gillem, Lt. Gen. Alvan C., Jr., 114
Gillespie, Maj. Gen. George L., 6
Glasby, Pvt., 73-75
Glass, Edward L. N., comments on Negroes as soldiers, 58
Gleaves, Lt. Albert, 51, 52
Grant, Capt. Joseph S., Jr., 119
Grant, Gen. Ulysses S., 20, 26
Gravely, Lt. Commander Samuel L., 118

135

Index

Greaves, Cpl. Clinton, 61-63
Grimes, James W., 3

Hall, Lt. Charles B., 112
Haman, Korea, 9, 11, 13
Harris, Sgt. James H., 29
Hartford, 45, 46, 48
Hawkins, Sgt. Maj. Thomas, 27
Hayward, Col. William, 100-101
Helicopter pilots, acts of bravery
    by, 120-121
Hell Fighters, 102
Henderson, Mary, 9-10
Henderson, Capt. Robert S., 120-
    121
Hennagan, Capt. Thomas L., 118-
    119
Hilton, Sgt. Alfred B., 30-32
Holland, Sgt. Maj. Milton M., 33
Holley, Air Force Capt. Keaver,
    III, 120
Hollis, Master Sgt. Levy V., 13
Honor, pyramid of, 8
Horner, Second Lt. Reuben, 110
Hudner, Lt. Thomas J., Jr., 14

Inchon, Korea, 11
Indian fighters, 57-83
*Integration and the Negro Officer
    in the Armed Forces*, 111-
    112
Italy, heroism of Negro helicop-
    ter pilots during floods in,
    120-121

James, Cpl. Miles, 33-34
James River flotilla, 40
John's Island, 35, 38
Johnson, Lt. C. P., 91
Johnson, Sgt. Henry, 68-70, 101-
    103
Johnson, Louis, 115
Johnson, Lyndon B., 124
Johnston, Capt. J. D., 48
Jones, Capt. James L., 111

Jordan, Sgt. George, 70, 71
Jumping Bull, 81

Kelly, First Sgt. Alexander, 32
Kennedy, John F., 119
    on discrimination in Armed
    Forces, 120
Kickapoo Springs, 60
Korean battlefields, 9-18, 116-118
Korean Service Medal, 15
Kuni-ri, Korea, 14

Lake Erie, battle of, 39
Las Guasimas, battle of, 87-90
Lawson, Landsman John, 45-48
Lee, Pvt. Fitz, 91-94, 98
Lee, Seaman James H., 43-44
Lee, Robert E., 21
Legáreville, S. C., 35
Lewis, Pvt., 79
Lindbergh, Brig. Gen. Charles
    A., 2
Lincoln, Abraham, 3
Liscome Bay, 109
Lockbourne Army Air Base, 112,
    115

McBryar, Sgt. William, 80-81
McClellan, Alonzo G., 50
McManus, Lt. Luther M., 17-18
Madison, Lt. John, 110
Manzanilla, Cuba, 98
Marine Corps, discrimination in,
    121
Marshall, Pvt., 97
Martin, Pvt., 75
Matsu, 117
Mays, Cpl. Isaiah, 12, 78-80
Meade, Lt. Commander Richard
    W., Jr., 35-36, 38
Medaille Militaire, 103
Medal of Honor, 1-7
    design of, 6-7
    list of recipients, 127-129
    review boards for, 4-5

Index

Membres Mountains of New Mexico, 63
Merimon, Cpl. Clifton, 104
Merrifield, Cpl. Ed, 103
Merrit, Gen. Wesley, 69
Meuse-Argonne offensive, 103-105, 111
Milk River siege, 68-70
Miller, Messman First Class Doris, 107-109
Minuteman missiles, 119
Mitchell, Maj. Gen. Ormsby M., 4
 raid through Georgia, 4
Mitchell, Maj. Gen. William C., 2
Morrow, Maj. Albert P., 66
Murphy, Pvt. Edward F., 67

Nana (Apache chief), 71, 73, 75-77
Navy Cross, 6, 109
Navy Medal of Honor, 3, 7, 40
 design of, 41
 first Negro seaman to receive, 38-39
Negro regiments, controversy over, in World War II, 105-106
New York Home for Homeless Boys, 10
New Market Heights, battle of, 28, 29, 34
New Orleans, capture of, 46
Nichols, Lee, 105
Nimitz, Chester W., 109
Ninety-ninth Pursuit Squadron, 107, 111, 112
Ninety-second Division, 100, 109, 110, 114
 adversities of, 103
Ninety-third Division, 100
Ninth Negro Cavalry, 58-59, 61, 63, 64, 66, 68, 71, 76, 80, 81, 84, 85, 94, 97, 99
Ninth Infantry Regiment, 14

Ninth Ohio Regiment, 94
Noil, Joseph B., 50, 56
Norfolk, Va., 50
Norton, Barney, 80

Ojo Caliente, N. M., 66
Olive, Pvt. First Class Milton L., III, 124-125
Olive, Milton L., II, letter of, 125

Pace, Frank, Jr., 17
Parham, Navy Capt. Thomas D., Jr., 121
Payne, Capt., 67
Pearl Harbor, 107-109
Pease, Joachim, 42-45
Penn, Robert, 53, 55
Perry, Commodore Oliver Hazard, 39, 42, 55
Pershing, Gen. John J., 106
Petersburg, battle of, 27-28
Phillips, Brig. Gen. Charles L., 101
Pine Ridge Agency, S. Dak., 81
Pinn, First Sgt. Robert, 33
Port Hudson, battle of, 46
Porter, First Lt. William E., 111
Purple Heart, 3, 6
"Pyramid of Honor," 8

Quemoy, 117

Ratcliff, First Sgt. Edward, 29
Review boards for Medal of Honor, 4-5
Rhode Island, first colored artillery regiment in, 21
Roberts, Pvt. Needham, 102, 103
Roosevelt, Franklin D., 107
Roosevelt, Theodore, 85, 87-90, 94, 97, 99
Rough Riders (First Volunteer Cavalry), 85, 88, 94, 97
Russell, Richard, 122

Index

San Carlos reservation, 61
San Juan Hill, 89, 90, 98
Santiago campaign of Spanish-American War, 84-98
Santiago de Cuba, 53, 97
Sea, Negroes at, 35-55
Selective Service Act, 107
Seventy-ninth Colored Infantry (First Kansas), 21
Silver Star, 6, 110, 111
Sioux campaign, 59, 81-83
Sitting Bull, 81
614th Tank Destroyer Battalion, 110
Sixth U. S. Colored Troops of Pennsylvania, 27, 30, 32
Smith, Fireman, 54
Smith, Lt. George W., 76
Smith, James W., 61
South Carolina State College, 61
Spanish-American War, 53
  discrimination during, 87
  Santiago campaign of, 84-98
Stance, Sgt. Emanuel, 59-61
Stanton, Edwin M., 4, 20
Steward, Theophilus Gould, 59
Stone River, 35
Strahan, Capt. of the Top Robert, 43
Stuckney, Asst. Engineer, 54
Sumner, Acting Master David H., 45
Suwon, Korea, 117

Tayabacoe heroes, 90-94, 98
Tennessee, 46, 48
Tenth Negro Cavalry, 58-59, 61, 80, 81, 83-86, 90, 94, 95, 97
Thirty-eighth U. S. Colored Troops, 29
Thirty-ninth U.S. Colored Troops, 28
Thirty-sixth U. S. Colored Troops, 29, 34

Thomas, Capt. Charles, 110
Thomas, Adjutant Gen. Lorenzo, 22
Thompkins, Pvt. William H., 91-94, 98
Thompson, Pvt. William, 9-12
Thornburgh, Maj. T. T., 66-67
369th Infantry Regiment, 100-102
  citations for, 104-105
366th Infantry Regiment, 111
332nd Fighter Group, 112, 113
  Distinguished Unit Citation to, 113
  Time magazine comments on, 112
Time magazine comments on 332nd Fighter Group, 112
Truman, Harry S., 12, 114, 116
Tuskegee Institute, 107
Twenty-fifth Negro Infantry, 58, 85
Twenty-first Infantry, 17-18
Twenty-fourth U. S. Cavalry, 78
Twenty-fourth Infantry Regiment, 9, 11, 12, 13, 15, 58, 85, 107

United Negro College Fund, 117
U. S. Department of Defense, 111
U. S. Manned Space Flight Program, 118
U. S. Military Academy (*see* West Point)
U. S. S. *Arizona*, 107, 109
U. S. S. *Cushing*, 51-53
U. S. S. *Falgout*, 118
U. S. S. *Iowa*, 53-55
U. S. S. *Kearsarge*, 42-44
U. S. S. *Leyte*, 14
U. S. S. *Marblehead*, 35, 42
U. S. S. *Powhatan*, 50
U. S. S. *Wyandank*, 48, 49
Ute Indians, battles with, 66-70

Index

Utilization of Negro Manpower in the Postwar Army, The, 114

Valois, Lt. Gustavus, 72, 73, 75
Van Alen, Cpl. Clarence R., 104
Veal, Pvt. Charles, 31, 32
Viareggio, 111
Vicksburg, battle of, 46
Victorio (Apache chief), 63-66, 70, 71
Vietnam war, 119, 124-125
    percentage of Negro casualties in, 121-123

Walker, Mary, 5
Wall, Sgt. John, 25
Walley, Pvt. Augustus, 72-75, 88-89
Walton, Boatswain J. C., 50
Wanton, Pvt. George H., 91-94, 98
Ware, Second Lt. William D., 13
Washington, George, 2
Watson, First Lt. J. W., 81

Welles, Gideon, 39-41
West Point, 94, 106
    first Negro graduate of, 61
Weyler, Valeriano, 86
Wham, Maj. J. W., 78-80
Wheeler, Gen. Earle G., 122-123
White Clay Creek, battle of, 82-83
Wilks, Commodore Charles, 40
Williams, First Sgt. Moses, 72-75
Williamson, Brig. Gen. Ellis W., 123
Wilson, Henry, 3
Wilson, Capt. John A., 42
Wilson, Sgt. William O., 57, 81-83
Wilson, Pvt., 73-75
Woods, Sgt. Brent, 70-77, 84
World War I, 100-106
World War II, 107-114
Wright, Lt. Henry H., 61, 63
Wynn, First Lt. Ellison C., 13

Yorktown, Pa., 23
Young, Maj. Charles D., 94

IRVIN H. LEE
Master Sergeant, U. S. Air Force

Irvin H. Lee was born in Baltimore, Maryland, and attended Morgan State College in that city. He joined the United States Air Force in 1952. Subsequently he served in the United States, Europe, and Asia as a military newspaper editor and magazine feature writer.

He is the author of many articles dealing with various subjects, both as a military man and free lance writer. These subjects have included religion, desegregation of the Armed Forces, missiles, guerilla warfare, and the American People-to-People Program. He is currently serving with the Joint Military Public Affairs Office, Military Assistance Command, Vietnam. Sergeant Lee has earned the Air Force Commendation Medal with two oak leaf clusters.